D0960142

PRAISE FOR *OUR FAVORITE SINS*

"In *Our Favorite Sins*, Hunter combines modern language and research with classic understanding in providing a fresh look and at our most deadly sins. His suggestions for 'ancient and fruitful' practices will be very helpful to many in reorienting desire toward living life with God."

—GARY W. MOON, M.DIV., PH.D., executive director,
Martin Family Institute and Dallas Willard Center
for Spiritual Formation, Westmont College;
author of *Apprenticeship with Jesus*

"One of the most persistent and least talked about questions for Christians are these: If sin is so bad, then why are we drawn to it? If it wrecks human lives—which it does, every time—then what is so appealing about its temptations? Is there any help for those who want to find freedom from sin? Todd Hunter has delved deeply into this matter, and in this excellent and accessible book Hunter offers us not only insight into why we sin, but how we can begin to turn from its false promises. The body of Christ needs this book."

—JAMES BRYAN SMITH,
author of *The Good and Beautiful God*

"The most deceptive part of sin is its ability to blind us to its reality in our lives. Todd Hunter offers sane and helpful guidance about the way out."

—JOHN ORTBERG, senior pastor, Menlo Park
Presbyterian Church; author of *The Me I Want to Be*

"It is so easy to miss our potential in life due to getting caught up in our weaknesses and temptations. Todd helps us understand not only how to recognize the subtle sins that can distract us, but how to be like Jesus when facing them."

—DAN KIMBALL, author of
They Like Jesus But Not the Church

"Todd Hunter draws on ancient practices in order to provide insight and strategy to face temptations in our lives. This book will help you think about how you can not just ask God to deliver you from temptation but be intentional about finding a way of escape."

—MARGARET FEINBERG, www.margaretfeinberg.com, author of *Scouting the Divine and The Sacred Echo*

"Todd Hunter gets it: Nothing should stand in the way of full devotion to Christ."

—BILL HYBELS, senior pastor, Willow Creek Community Church; chairman, Willow Creek Association

"This book speaks powerfully to some of my own deepest spiritual struggles. In offering candid, informed counsel on 'our favorite sins,' Todd Hunter has given me, and multitudes like me, an important spiritual treasure."

—DR. RICHARD MOUW, president, Fuller Seminary; author of *Praying at Burger King*

"Todd Hunter is the only man I know who can talk about sin with an appealing easiness and, at the time, with an equally appealing candor. I can almost guarantee that you'll enjoy his conversation and end up very grateful for having had the chance to read it."

—PHYLLIS TICKLE, author of *The Great Emergence*

"One of the greatest intellectual achievements of the Christian tradition is its notion of original sin. People will make a mess of anything, of everything. Todd Hunter has gifted us with an inspiring book that suggests habits of holiness for everyday living and moving and having our being amid human suckitude and stinkiness. But most of all, Bishop Hunter gives us hope that "where sin abounded, grace did much more abound."

—LEONARD SWEET, best-selling author, professor, and chief contributor to sermons.com

OUR
FAVORITE
SINS

OUR FAVORITE SINS

The Sins We Commit & How You Can Quit

TODD D. HUNTER

THOMAS NELSON
Since 1798

NASHVILLE   DALLAS   MEXICO CITY   RIO DE JANEIRO

© 2012 by Todd Hunter

All rights reserved. No portion of this book may be reproduced, stored in a retrieval system, or transmitted in any form or by any means—electronic, mechanical, photocopy, recording, scanning, or other—except for brief quotations in critical reviews or articles, without the prior written permission of the publisher.

Published in Nashville, Tennessee, by Thomas Nelson. Thomas Nelson is a registered trademark of Thomas Nelson, Inc.

Thomas Nelson, Inc., titles may be purchased in bulk for educational, business, fundraising, or sales promotional use. For information, please e-mail SpecialMarkets@ThomasNelson.com.

Unless otherwise noted, Scripture quotations are taken from HOLY BIBLE: NEW INTERNATIONAL VERSION®. © 1973, 1978, 1984 by Biblia, Inc.™ Used by permission of Zondervan Worldwide. All rights reserved. www.zondervan.com

Scripture quotations marked MSG are from *The Message* by Eugene H. Peterson. © 1993, 1994, 1995, 1996, 2000. Used by permission of NavPress Publishing Group. All rights reserved.

Scripture quotations marked KJV are from the KING JAMES VERSION.

Scripture quotations marked NLT are from *Holy Bible*, New Living Translation. © 1996. Used by permission of Tyndale House Publishers, Inc., Wheaton, Illinois 60189. All rights reserved.

Scripture quotations marked AMPLIFIED BIBLE are from THE AMPLIFIED BIBLE: OLD TESTAMENT. ©1962, 1964 by Zondervan (used by permission); and from THE AMPLIFIED BIBLE: NEW TESTAMENT. © 1958 by the Lockman Foundation (used by permission).

Scripture quotations marked CEV are from THE CONTEMPORARY ENGLISH VERSION. © 1991 by the American Bible Society. Used by permission.

Scripture quotations marked NKJV are from THE NEW KING JAMES VERSION. © 1982 by Thomas Nelson, Inc. Used by permission. All rights reserved.

Scripture quotations marked NASB are from NEW AMERICAN STANDARD BIBLE®; © The Lockman Foundation 1960, 1962, 1963, 1968, 1971, 1972, 1973, 1975, 1977, 1995. Used by permission.

Library of Congress Cataloging-in-Publication Data

Hunter, Todd D., 1956-
 Our favorite sins : the sins we commit and how you can quit / Todd Hunter.
  pages cm
 Includes bibliographical references.
 ISBN 978-1-59555-444-4
1. Sins. 2. Christian life. I. Title.
 BV4625.H86 2012
 241'.3--dc23

2011048461

Printed in the United States of America

12 13 14 15 16 QG 6 5 4 3 2 1

For Jacqueline Rae Hunter.
Passing through life's patches of dense,
disorienting fog, she made her way to the Light,
becoming light, love, and strength to those she loved.

CONTENTS

CONTENTS

FOREWORD

Walking out of our favorite sins makes perfect sense after you have done it. But you need a biblical, psychologically sophisticated, pastoral guide to get you to that point. That is Todd Hunter. Sin is basically stupid and repulsive. But when you are in its snare—few aren't—you can't see that. The best thing about *Our Favorite Sins* is, it really does enable you to see sin for what it is. And then it gives small doable steps you can take to walk away.

Do you want to quit? You can. Just meditatively study this book and put it, gently but persistently, into practice. Don't worry about perfection. If you ever get there, it will be safe for you. It's when you aren't there that it is dangerous—deadly! This book will do wonders for serious disciples of Jesus, and it would be great for small groups. But we're talking world revolution here, which is exactly what Jesus had in mind: "Teach the disciples to do everything I said." What else is there to do?

DALLAS WILLARD

ONE

THE TYRANNY OF WHAT YOU WANT

*O wretched man that I am! Who will
deliver me from this body of death?*

—ROMANS 7:24 NKJV

Over the year that I worked on this book, I encountered
friends and family members who asked what I was working
on. When I told them about the content of *Our Favorite Sins*,
they often raised an eyebrow while lowering their gaze and
said things like, "Why? Are *you* an authority?" Or, "I always
had my suspicions about *you*!" Or, "I didn't even know what
sin was till I met *you*!"

Maybe, like me, you've had a long-standing fear of being
exposed as less than superspiritual. One thought, one fear, has
been nagging like a demon in the back of my mind while writing this book. It is this: there has been some sort of cosmic

WikiLeak of the books in heaven and now everyone knows Todd Hunter is an expert on temptation.

The truth is I do have great experience fighting temptation. I have always been radically tempted by selfishness, though I doubt many would suspect it. I am widely known among my friends and colleagues as a loving, kind, and generous person. People think of me as modest, humble, and soft-spoken. But these qualities do not come to me naturally. If I have any of these qualities, they come from decades of battling radical, deeply rooted pride. What's the disconnect between what I experience inwardly and what others observe outwardly? In a word, *struggle*. Fighting the good fight. An inward resistance and journey not visible to anyone but God.

I think anyone who is conscious of temptation and sin intuitively knows this. We are all familiar with not only the words but also the feeling expressed by the apostle Paul in Romans: "O wretched man that I am! Who will deliver me from this body of death?" (7:24 NKJV).

Before Paul there was Samson, the famous leader of Israel. Though he was given miraculous power to carry out the will of God, Samson fell headlong for Delilah. Israel's enemies immediately used their knowledge of Samson's desire to their benefit. They bribed and manipulated Delilah so that, while Samson lay in her lap, she coaxed the secret of his supernatural strength from him. It was just that easy. He was undone, captured.

You've probably had the experience of being utterly enthralled by a story. It's like you're present in the scene. You can smell the aromas. You can touch the people. The story of Samson has that effect on me. As his weakness is revealed, his bloody eye sockets oozing at the end of a Philistine spear, I can hear him saying, "Wretched man that I am! Who will deliver me from this body of death?"

Then there's David and Bathsheba. David, while walking on his roof, saw Bathsheba bathing. Bathsheba was the wife of another man. But when the moment was on, that little detail did not seem to bother David. Dazzled, David desired Bathsheba. Then he had her and impregnated her. To cover his sin, David called home Bathsheba's husband, one of his loyal soldiers, for a conjugal visit with Bathsheba. But the man refused to abandon his comrades. Desperate and without options, David arranged to have the man killed in battle. With her husband out of the way, David then married Bathsheba. She eventually delivered the child of their adultery, but the boy soon died; his death, as the prophet Nathan foretold, was the consequence of David's sin. I can almost hear David's anguished cry as he watched his son die: "Wretched man that I am! Who will deliver me . . . ?"

It's a Struggle

Beating temptation requires struggle because it always involves sorting out rightly ordered desires for good and godly things from our disordered desires for wrong things. We often experience these disordered desires as our most powerful and deeply rooted desires. Uprooting disordered desires involves personal, psychological, and spiritual suffering.[1] But this death produces life, life, and more life—life more abundant. However, a journey of focused, grace-enabled struggle is required to get there. Dietrich Bonhoeffer, an honored saint, explains why: "In [the parts of our bodies] there is a slumbering inclination towards desire that is both sudden and fierce. With irresistible power desire seizes mastery over the flesh. All at once a secret, smoldering fire is kindled . . . [and] the lust thus aroused envelops the mind and will of man in the deepest darkness. The powers of clear discrimination and of decision are taken from us."[2]

We've all had our particular Delilahs, our individual Bathshebas. They're not all sexual temptations, either. Not by a long shot. There are innumerable ways to gratify our desires that are contrary to God's will for our lives. We all give in to temptation, don't we? In strolls our Delilah, up charges our desire, and out comes a string of rationalizations to justify our sin. It is sad and bizarre that we indulge our flesh even for a moment, after which we're sure to feel guilty and ashamed. The Holy Spirit in us says one thing, and our conscience echoes it. But everything else in us fights and argues and rationalizes.

It goes something like this: *I, in this case, with this set of facts, am the exception. Given the totality of my circumstances and experiences, this isn't really a sin, not actually, not in this way, not if you really look at it from the right angle. I can fulfill this one particular desire. It's not really a Big Sin, Major Sin, or Bad Sin.*

You know how it goes. And it makes sense in the moment. But like a friend of mine used to say, "Sin makes you stupid."

Then the trouble starts. Problems at work, at school, with the kids, or with a spouse. That muted conscience raises its voice. Then you find that the guy, the gal, the substance, the experience is really not all that after all. Not too far down the path, if God is still with you, if he has not given you over to your sin (Romans 1:24–28), you realize that somewhere you really did lose coherent and good judgment, the ability to make clearheaded decisions. Sin robs us of our clarity.

Scripture says that God has given us the power of a sound mind (2 Timothy 1:7). The New International Version calls this sound mind "self-discipline." The idea is that God gives to those who ask and seek for it the ability to be conscious of and sensible about our desires. Any clarity we have is a foot-hold given by God to begin the fight, to begin the resistance that leads to life. Giving in to disordered desire has only one outcome: death.

That's why the apostle Paul counseled so often and so strongly that we flee from sin and temptation (see, for instance, 1 Corinthians 6:18; 10:14; 1 Timothy 6:11; 2 Timothy 2:22). And James, the brother of Jesus himself, said that if we resist the devil, the tempter, he'll flee from us (James 4:7). Sin always brings struggle. But rather than struggling against the Spirit and our conscience, we need to strive *with* them, recruiting them as all-purpose foot soldiers in the fight against sin and temptation.

I know this battle firsthand. Any good that others see in me comes from an intense inner struggle over several decades. This is not a struggle *against* God but a struggle *with* God against my disordered desires, my default position of radical selfishness. God is *with* me in this struggle because he wants my transformation more than I want it. I simply cooperate with him. Together we reorder my desires.

Disordered Desire

There are a few thoughts we'll want to keep in mind as we move forward.

First, there is a condition that each of us lives with and from which we struggle to be freed. Think of it as a person's system of desires, thoughts, feelings, will, and heart in a state of disorder. We live in a posture of misalignment with the purposes of God for humanity. The Bible calls this condition spiritual death. Spiritual life, on the other hand, is most simply described as God's spirit and our spirit in alignment and in harmony, made one by the atoning, forgiving, regenerating power of God in Christ Jesus.

Second, we've seen the stories of two men who acted, behaved, and made choices from the place of spiritual death within them. But you should note: Samson and David were not merely spiritually dead. Both had a real spiritual life and walked with God. Both show up in the New Testament hall of fame. Though flawed, they are celebrated as persons of commendable faith (Hebrews 11). That is the lesson for us: we all have within us two natures, what Paul calls the old and new man. The old is the one whose desires are misaligned. These disordered desires, as we'll see, give birth to sin.

Third, temptation is always produced by desire. Samson desired something so much that he tossed aside his desire to live in obedient partnership with God. Delilah had something he wanted so badly that his desire for her caused his desire for God and God's purposes to fade into the background.

Similar observations could be made about David and his desire for Bathsheba. He crossed numerous moral, religious, spiritual, professional, and military lines in order to have what he desired. As David's life went on he discovered that, in actual surprising fact, his desires also *had* him. They had him in their clutches. Disordered desires are a tyrant. This is why we struggle against them, striving to overthrow them in our hearts like the little despots they are.

Unfortunately, many of us don't even know what we're up against. In researching temptation I had David Kinnaman and the Barna Group conduct a survey to help me get a gauge for how we think and act when faced with life's various enticements. I will be referring to these exclusive findings as we make our way through the book, and you can refer to the summary of this study in the appendix.

Here's one startling finding up front: 50 percent of Americans simply don't know what to do about temptation. Picture it: I'm standing in line at the store with nine other people; five of us have no idea what to do should the clerk give us too much change or verbalize an inappropriate come-on. Or I'm sitting at the movies or at a concert, nine others in my row; five of us don't have a productive, effective thought or positive design for handling what we may see or hear. Is it any wonder we find it difficult to control ourselves, to stop sinning? Our disordered desires are ruling our hearts and minds, and we don't know what to do about it.

My experience as a pastor for over thirty years tells me that most people cannot win a victory over many things that matter in their lives, whether these things are spousal relations, child rearing, dance, golf, their favorite art, their favorite hobby, or sin. My decades as a pastor and leader in various capacities in sports, at work, at schools, in nonprofits, and in churches tell me that many Christians are at their wits' end. Casting themselves on the love and forgiveness of God, but forgetting his call to discipleship, many have decided to "just keep it real" and to "just be who they are" and to "not worry about what others think or how others might judge them." "Wretched man that I am," you can almost hear them saying, and maybe you've said with them, "I give up."

It makes a certain sort of sense. Who could or would want to argue against "keeping it real" and the amazing love and forgiveness of God? What else are we going to do? After all, the reasoning goes, we are only human. Those sentiments are popular and seemingly reasonable. But in truth, giving up and "keeping it real" versus trying and failing is actually a false dualism of the worst kind. Yet the vast majority of people who think this way are not in fact trying to live a lie. They feel defeated and they just don't see any other choice.

I've got good news: despite all our failures and shameful "moments after," we are not stuck between a life that makes us hate ourselves on the one hand and feel the love of God on the other. There is a third way. A whole new approach—which is actually old, tested, and true in practice—awaits.

Temptation Is a Fact

This book is about all of us. It is about how we struggle with desire, how we resist temptation and sin. In the pages that follow I try to leverage a long life of working with myself and others in order to shine a revealing light on temptation for contemporary readers. While the Barna data takes all Americans into account, *Our Favorite Sins* is lovingly written to encourage those who have decided to resist those favorite sins, those of us looking for ways to "win" against temptation. Someone who has lost the category of *sin*, someone who does not believe that something like *sin* exists, is not likely to appreciate the exploration of desire and temptation that is found in the pages ahead.

People don't slip up and, looking back, find that they were following Jesus and growing in their ability to make godly discernments and sound moral judgments. But every day hundreds of millions of people drift into choices, decisions, and habits that destroy their lives, families, social networks, classrooms, workplaces, and more. Achieving victory over temptation and sin, even with all God does and supplies to ensure our success, requires intentionality and purpose on our part. It also requires that we know what we're really fighting.

The times change, and temptation changes with them. Christians struggle with challenges today that are unique to our culture and decade. And as times change, beliefs and assumptions do as well. God's purposes don't change, but the ways we are beguiled into deviating from his purposes surely do. Because the things that tempt or test us change, followers of Jesus are often caught by surprise.

Once all the societal changes are sifted, one rock of truth is left lying on the bottom of the sieve: *temptation is a fact*. It just *is*: in all times and all places. The fact of temptation is one of the rare truths that do not change with the times. The story of Adam and Eve, who wanted more than what they had been given, is our story today, just as it was for generations in the centuries past. But the Serpent keeps up with technological change, and the apple evolves in a million different ways from one generation to the next, one decade to the next. Eve never coveted Adam's smartphone, and Adam never heard of a centerfold, let alone a downloadable digital one.

Cultures change, and the species of temptation change with them. Americans struggle with things today that are unique to our culture, time, and place. No book on temptation written fifty years ago would have dealt with possible addiction to video games. No sermon or article on temptation from ten years ago would have mentioned addiction to social media such as Facebook, YouTube, and Twitter.

As times and temptations change, beliefs and assumptions about them shift as well. What one generation of Americans considers a virtue another generation considers a vice. The hard work of my generation (the baby boomers) has largely been rejected by the next generation in favor of a more balanced life that makes space for friends, family, and recreation. The same pattern holds true for churchgoers who, in the space of one generation, have come to tolerate sins that a previous generation would not have condoned. For instance, few people seem to wring their hands anymore about divorce. Except for the most notorious cases involving abuse or sexual scandal, it is for the most part accepted, even in the church.

More Like Joseph

Paul, in a moment of self-reflection, once observed that he was "a wretched man." We all know and feel his exasperation. But it need not defeat us or play out in a David-like or Samson-like way in our life. There is a better way. Once you make one major, inner move, you can find the exit door from temptation most of the time. Joseph, the son of the patriarch Jacob, shows us how. Famous for his coat of many colors, his dreams, and his jealous siblings, Joseph had something much more critical: rightly ordered desires.

Joseph's life is a picture of the good, the beautiful, and the true. Inviting readers into such a life through rightly ordered desires is the goal of this book. There is a larger discussion of Joseph in the conclusion, but for now let's trace the large outlines of his life.

Because of the calling and blessing of God, everything Joseph did prospered. His various supervisors at work respected, valued, and admired him. He was handsome and well built. When his boss's wife took notice of him and asked him to go to bed with her, he refused. Why? Here is Joseph's answer: *I am doing work for God. He is prospering my work. This prosperous work is necessary for the well-being of many people. I cannot injure this relationship and thwart this task.* That was Joseph's mind-set. Not that it slowed his boss's wife down.

His boss's wife continued to pursue Joseph. Many times she tried to lure him into sex with her. His consistent rebuttal gives us a vision for defeating temptation the way a clean window yields an unambiguous view on a bright, clear day: *How could I do such a wicked thing and sin against God?* Making God and his calling and purpose for our life *primary*, the first and highest-held desire of our life, is the path to freedom. It is the strong deliverer from the tyranny of what we want, the reordering principle for our disordered desires. Joseph resisted temptation, and though he faced trials and difficulties, he triumphed through his sound mind-set. It was given him by the grace and favor of God. But make no mistake: he cooperated in that God-process. In this book I'll show you how to cooperate in a similar manner.

Contrast Joseph's story and the mental image it creates with the reality experienced by most of us. According to the Barna research, 59 percent of Americans say that the last time they were faced with temptation, they did nothing specific to avoid giving in to it. Joseph resisted. Joseph ran. We, on the other hand, do nothing. We need help. We need tools. We need the right equipment to get in the game.

I hope to pass on some usable tools in the pages to come. After finishing *Our Favorite Sins*, you should be equipped to battle the temptations you face with a new, unique, and empowering perspective on sin, temptation, and desire. I want to give you the confidence to know that while your particular temptations may seem unique, you actually share a strong bond with believers of the past. There really is a great cloud of witnesses testifying to us about how to get victory over temptation.

Once we come to grips with the fact that our real enemy is our own internal disordered desires, we can work on reordering those desires. And that great cloud of witnesses testifies to a real, workable, effective path to do exactly that. Ancient, liturgical, and sacramental forms of Christian spirituality can assist a follower of Jesus in defeating temptation and gaining victory over sin by training and conditioning us to reorder our desires.

An Invitation

Some sins are easily visible, like hitting an innocent person. Some are less so, like a hidden attitude of hatred. Most of the temptations and sins we will deal with in the pages of this book are the ones that are most readily seen and measured. We need to take this approach for concreteness of exploration, explanation, and growth. But there is a downside. You may not see your particular temptation listed. You may not relate precisely to the stories I tell about myself. But don't be put off or alarmed. The principles we draw from the specific research and personal stories are easily applied to your specific set of desires, temptations, and sins.

While this book has a distinctly Christian point of view in terms of the origin of common daily temptations, and while it offers historic Christian weapons against temptation, anyone can learn from this book. Truth is truth. Help is help. Guidance is guidance. Wisdom and effective practices are just that. One should not, in my view, reject workable solutions for temptations just because they come from Jesus or his first followers. Falling to temptation hurts us all, not just Christians but Jews, Muslims, Buddhists, and atheists too. Yielding to temptation is all-inclusive in its effect. There is no such thing as private sin. We are in fact social creatures by design, birth, and choice.

The sin that results from desire and temptation is like a major earthquake in deep ocean waters. We think we can hide it because it is underwater, but this strategy never works. It never stays underwater. Earthquakes of sin always cause tsunamis of destruction: a wall of fast-moving water that swamps homes, obliterates factories, destroys farmers' fields, drowns the books in libraries, and smashes boats and cars on the pilings of bridges. Nothing and no one in its path goes untouched. This is the true social and public nature of sin—and the desires and temptations that proceed and produce it. Sin is not just a religious term or idea. It touches all of us. That is why we should all care, whether we are religious or not.

When we turn the page to chapter 2, we will explore what temptation is and how it interacts with desire to produce sin. In chapter 3 we will discover what we say about temptation according to the latest research. In later chapters we will discover the historic, tried, and proven methods of reordering our desires and dealing with temptation. We will conclude by putting all these ingredients together in an effort to be delivered from *the tyranny of what we want*.

There are at least a few notions from the Scriptures that lead us to intelligently fight temptation. God calls us to live holy lives. Jesus says to be holy. Peter echoes his Lord and God, calling for holiness as well. Paul calls us to live holy lives that are pleasing to God. John says that we are to walk not in darkness but in the light of Jesus, keeping his commands, and, perhaps most famously, that we are not to love the world or the things of the world. If you've been in the church for any time at all, you've heard this line of thought. And we want to respond appropriately, mostly, most of the time. But we don't live up to that holy standard and usually feel helpless to really change in any permanent way. Guilt follows—maybe shame. Soon after, the intention to be different wilts under the relentless negativity of self-deprecation, humiliation, and remorse.

Are we consigned to defeat? Is there really a possibility for new life wherein we are not controlled by and victimized by our desires? If, as Paul said, "the wages of sin is death," let's find our way to a new way of living, to a fresh way of being, to "the gift of God," which is "eternal life in Jesus Christ our Lord" (Romans 6:23 NKJV).

Maybe we could begin small, with something doable, with a simple prayer asking God to make us conscious that he is always with us in twin ways, like an umpire seeing and judging and like the Good Physician diagnosing and healing that which the umpire scrutinizes. The prayer I suggest below can get you started if you don't know where else to begin.

Ancient and Fruitful Practice

Sit with the prayer below for a few quiet moments. Try to connect with its central petition. Begin to use this as an all-purpose prayer when temptation comes up in your life.

A Collect for Guidance: *Heavenly Father, in you we live and move and have our being: We humbly pray you so to guide and govern us by your Holy Spirit, that in all the cares and occupations of our lives we may not forget you, but may remember that we are ever walking in your sight; through Jesus Christ our Lord.* Amen.[3]

TWO

DISORDERED
DESIRES

*Keep away from worldly desires that
wage war against your very souls.*
—1 PETER 2:11 NLT

I'd just taken a few steps out the front door of church after a Sunday worship service when a friend, Bob, walked up to me with gusto and, with a joyous smile, said, "Now there's temptation right there!" He was pointing to a shiny, black, brand-new Harley-Davidson motorcycle in the parking lot about twenty yards away. A few guys were slowly sauntering around it, admiring the Harley look and vibe.

I have a strong rule of thumb to never be preachy in off-hand conversations. But in this case, because my friend has a great sense of humor and since I had the concept of temptation at the very front of my mind while I worked on this book, I blurted out before my vow could stop me: "That is not temptation to me at all, Bob." Bob looked at me with great disappointment. I think we were both a bit sad that I did not share his ecstasy at the sight of a Harley. Even worse, it was like I'd just said the earth was flat or the sky was green. I went on to explain that temptation doesn't derive its power from what I see with my eyes, that *I can be tempted only when a desire I already have within me matches something that comes to my attention.*

Like most people, I instantly recognize the Harley logo and look. The logo is everywhere: on jackets, T-shirts, purses, mall stores, and belt buckles. And to the extent that I care about motorcycles, which isn't much, I do think Harleys look cool.

But I have no interest in *riding* motorcycles. I am not sure why, but I've never once in my life wished I could own or ride a motorbike. If I lived in a quaint European village, I might be able to see myself riding a Vespa to work and back or from home to the store a couple of blocks away. But even that may just be a daydream I would never act on.

Maybe I don't like motorcycles because people in my life have been seriously injured on them. Maybe I don't think the wind blowing through my hair is worth the bugs in my teeth. Whatever the reason, all I know is that I told Bob the truth. Even the hippest Harley does not tempt me, not even in the slightest. *But*, I thought as we stood there looking at the Harley, *if that were an amazing-looking woman undressing in public, or a German chocolate cake, it would get my attention!*

That story sets forth a crucial bit of knowledge regarding temptation. I mentioned it above, but being the core insight of this book, it bears repeating: something tempts me only if there is a preexisting desire in me for the object in view. Sin and temptation are powerless without my desires.

I'd bet my last dollar that had Bob not enthusiastically pointed out the Harley, I would have walked to my car a hundred times and never noticed it. Not so a woman disrobing in public. Of that sight I would be keenly aware. I'd feel adrenaline instantly jolt through my body. I'd have to employ my conscious mind to do the right thing, to look away. Why? I have a long (since puberty), deep (so deep that I cannot dig enough to find it), and constant desire for the opposite sex. That's how I'm wired, and that awareness is essential for battling the temptations that beset me. The same thing applies however you happen to be wired. Temptation does not produce desire. Desire makes temptation possible. To beat temptation, I need to reorder my desires.

The real sources of temptation do not come from hip, inviting marketing slogans from businesses like the Ritz-Carlton: "Some appetites are meant to be spoiled . . ."[1] The actual starting place for temptation lies deep within us.

Predator or Prey?

Our disordered desires beat the tar out of us. They flick us around life the way we snap a flea off our arm and send it flying across the room. Like powerful addictions, they cause us to deceive and betray the ones we love most in this world. They lead us to actions that put our jobs or careers in jeopardy. Through them we can rationalize almost any behavior or decision. They stomp all over what little character we do have with unrelenting energy that rivals the cast of *Stomp* beating push brooms and clomping their boots on a large, loud stage.

You know your desires are leading you into trouble when you repeatedly say things like this to yourself:

- If I just had her/him—the ideal spouse—instead of my present wife/husband, I know I would be happy.
- If I could just get this promotion, it would fix everything in my unhappy life.
- If I were just thin enough, he/she would notice me.
- My meaningless life could be put right if only I had more money, power, prestige, or significance.
- Gratifying this desire will give me a sense of self-worth, the sense that I matter and that my life has significance.
- I will go into total panic mode, I will lose complete control of myself, if I cannot get what I desire.

Take it from two of Jesus' best friends: the role of desire in the human person is a big deal. James said, "If all you want is your own way, flirting with the world every chance you get, you end up enemies of God and his way" (James 4:4 MSG). Peter said, "As obedient children, do not conform to the evil desires you had when you lived in ignorance . . . I urge you . . . to abstain from sinful desires, which wage war against your soul" (1 Peter 1:14; 2:11).

Here are a couple of big questions to help you discern whether or not, as James and Peter say, a desire is evil and sinfully disordered: Do you use the person or thing as a way to escape reality? Do you use the object desired to medicate pain in your life? When you do so, do you find the decision was, in the end, irrational and destructive in light of the bigger goals in your life? Are you mad at God? Do you feel like your unhappiness, your disappointment, has a "god" (whatever that may be) dimension to it? Do you feel like this god has somehow let you down? If so, this is a big hurdle to assess and conquer right here at the beginning of our work together. Here is why: the only way out of the mess of our disordered desires is to reorient and realign our whole lives around God and what he is up to on earth. When the time comes that we see God and his loving, grace-filled invitation to be his cooperative friends in this life and the life to come, we will have then found the potential to disconnect our hearts and intentions from wrong desires. Without such trust in God rooted in deep and sincere belief in his goodness, none of us are likely to take the journey suggested in this book.

Not rejecting but accepting the reality of God is the first step—but even this step is only a potential step. And nothing, as the old saying goes, is more common than unfulfilled potential. To realize that potential, we need to cash the check, so to speak, that God has written us. We need to act. We'll get to action later in the book. For now, so we understand where we are going in this book, let's further explore the tyranny of what we want, of strong desire or lust.

"Lust is the inordinate passion of un-integrated desire for pleasure, often sexual pleasure, power or money."[2] Someone close to you, a loved one, is right now in the vise grip of such disordered desire. I'll bet you can easily call this person to mind. Is it a parent you are seeing? A close friend? Your sister or brother? We have only to stop and think for a brief moment to recognize friends and family members whose lives are trapped in the functional equivalent of the coils of a boa constrictor. The boa, lying in wait under a bush, caught them as they walked by for the umpteenth time on their way to their favorite vendor of What They Want.

For months or years now, you've observed that your loved one is in the coils of something unrelenting. Over time you've watched the snake of What They Want coil ever tightly around, causing them and their life to become a scary shade of bluish purple. Whether *they* are in denial or not, *you* can see it: they are soon to be swallowed as prey.

And let's be frank: maybe that person is you.

Is it too much to say that a lot of American life, and that of the developed world, is in such a predicament? Based on my experience helping people of all kinds and all ages, I think not. What we pastors, therapists, counselors, teachers, supervisors, and managers have intuitively known for ages is demonstrably true: millions of people think they are looking for something, when in fact they are being looked for—they are becoming prey.

Our Top Temptations

What are the top five self-reported temptations in America?[3] According to the Barna survey:[4]

1. Sixty percent of Americans are often or sometimes living in a state of noticeable and debilitating temptation to anxiety or worry, and the fear and dysfunction that usually come with it.[5] The younger you are, the more probable it is that you are stuck in the rut of apprehension about life.[6]

2. Sixty percent of Americans are often or sometimes stuck in habits of procrastination.[7] We simply cannot do what needs to be done in a timely manner. Again, this is more a temptation for the young than for their grandparents.[8]

3. Fifty-five percent are often or sometimes overwhelmed by the temptation to eat too much.[9] Overeating and the growing concern about obesity is of course not news. A quick click on Google turns up 7.6 million hits for the word *obesity*. In recent months I've noticed many major news outlets running features on the growing alarm concerning overeating and obesity.

4. Forty-four percent of Americans admit that they face temptations to overuse electronics and social media such as Facebook, video games, and television.[10] Young people are almost twice as likely as their elders to become addicted to online activities. But this should not lead one to assume that their parents (boomers) and grandparents (elders) are immune from the temptation. I am a boomer, and I have plenty of friends who have negative consequences in their lives because they cannot tear themselves away from their phones or laptops.

5. Forty-one percent of Americans say they are often or sometimes tempted by laziness or by not working as hard as reasonably expected in their occupations.[11] All of the generations that Barna polled are about the same when it comes to the temptation to slothfulness. Selfishness is a core sin within humankind. Perhaps that explains why people of all ages are tempted to hurt family, friends, coworkers, and bosses with selfish slacking, doing what feels good to them however much it may harm others.

Anxiety, procrastination, overeating, Internet and social media, and laziness: these are some of the most real issues of life. At any given place and time, say the busy sidewalks of a college campus or the busy lunchroom of a large software company, you could draw a circle around half the people in those places and thereby give yourself a great visual image of the pain, frustration, dysfunction, and destruction caused by our failure to understand and cope well with temptation.

Maybe you didn't see your besetting temptation in the top five. Don't worry. Failures with temptation are not rooted in their type or category. Human temptation has so many variables, versions, and combinations that no list could contain all of them. Consider one easy temptation that surprisingly does not show up on the list: disordered sex. The unique ways in which it manifests itself in human society are nearly endless; there are almost as many ways as there are people—six billion! So don't look to the list itself for help. The crucial, fundamental strategy is to look within, at what you want, crave, covet, and desire. From there we'll see how to rearrange those desires to fit within the story of God and your role within it. And the strategies and insights we gain from studying one temptation are almost always applicable to every other temptation because temptations of all kinds have a common root.

Feed Me!

Let's take a little pause here. Have you ever thought about tyranny and desire together before? Have you ever put those two words together in a sentence? Have you ever seen them used together in a sentence? I'll never forget the first time I saw them together. It was arresting, as in put-the-book-down, "wow" arresting. The sentence said something I knew intuitively was true for me, and in that moment I realized I had seen the same tyrannizing effects on others. But I had never seen these effects as clearly as when I read for the first time 1 Peter 4:1–2 in Eugene Peterson's paraphrase of the Bible, *The Message*: "Think of your sufferings as a weaning from that old sinful habit of *always expecting to get your own way*. Then you'll be able to live out your days free to pursue what God wants instead of being *tyrannized by what you want*" (emphasis added).

But temptation, getting my way, and obtaining what I want never feel like the doorway to tyranny. Most of the time temptation begins with something good: food, rest, God-approved sex, the need to be loved and accepted. We could go on. Perhaps this is why the first sensation is always one of anticipation, of potential happiness and of greater personal fulfillment. Right? The mind controlled by lust, by *epithumia* (the New Testament Greek word for "strong desires or passions"), has an infinite capacity for rationalization. Let me call to mind here some bits of common thinking, a few thoughts we have all used at one point or another:

- He/she/it makes me feel alive—makes me feel the most *me*!
- How can something that feels so right be wrong?
- God wants me to be happy. This makes me happy at the core of my being. How can this be wrong?
- I'm acting out of love—I love her/him!
- My marriage was never the perfect will of God— he/she is my true soul mate!
- I'm the exception to the rule . . . in my case, I don't think anything bad will happen to *me*.
- The people who do not approve of what I am doing are just judgmental nags—they make me sick! They are worse than I am![12]

Think about the attempts at validation you just read. What do they mean? What do they teach us? I think they are a deep and profound glimpse into the power of rationalization for those who are being tyrannized by their own desires. Our structures of desire can become so out of control that, according to our honest experiences of life, our *desires* become our most concrete and real feelings and experiences. In time, with the tyranny unchecked, you learn from your experience that *there is no me apart from gratifying my desires—fulfilling my system of desire equals me.* The honest feeling becomes this: *I am my desires.* Or *I will be the real me when my desires are fulfilled.*

But that kind of life is heartbreaking and delusional. Giving into our desires only strengthens them. This is positive news if the desires are good and holy. It's one of the ways we grow in the grace of God. But if the desires are out of whack, our disordered desire takes greater and greater control of our lives, and we can fall farther and farther into sin.

Do you recall the rock-and-roll musical *Little Shop of Horrors?* One of the lead characters, Seymour, worked in a floral shop. There was one plant that was fed only on blood. But the blood was never enough. The plant kept growing and demanding more. Maybe you recall the lines: "Feed me Seymour . . . feed me now! I'm starving! Feed me Seymour all night long!" That is exactly the state of affairs for those who are caught in the tyranny of their desires. They can never give themselves enough of their habit—sex, food, drugs, drink, or money—to satisfy themselves. And our culture doesn't help.

Unrelenting Stimuli

Popular visual media of all kinds—web, print, and television—have filled our eyes to such an astonishing degree that it makes actually fulfilling desire almost impossible. Though the stimuli outstrip even our most intense desires, and even though we could never experience the entire rainbow of stimuli, we keep trying. As we do, we exhaust ourselves physically and spiritually and cause distress to those closest to us.

If we stop here for a moment to think about it, I bet you'll agree with me that nothing lives up to the images. For instance, in the seventies, when I was a teenager, I worked for the City of Anaheim at Angel Stadium. I was one of those guys who walked around in a bright orange smock with a broom and dustpan sweeping up cracked and discarded peanut shells and mopping up beer spills. Being at the stadium for every game, I got used to seeing an occasional famous person.

All the middle-aged guys can agree with me about this fact: the seventies was the decade of the famous poster of Farrah Fawcett. I hear she was a wonderful woman and did not deserve to be treated as an object. But at the time I did not know any better. Neither did I know what lighting, makeup artists, and airbrushing did to the woman we wrongly objectified.

I was so disappointed the night I saw her. She was very attractive, but not light-years more so than other attractive women. Something of the magic was missing. The lust stimulated by the poster could not deal with the normal beauty of reality. Shame on me for objectifying a woman for my own desires—and shame on the many media industries that forty years later are still selling artificial stimuli that can never satisfy.

But that cautionary disgrace does not keep millions of people and thousands of vendors from trying. Thus the hole in which we now stand is almost so deep, so darkened by the shadow of unfulfilled desire, that we can no longer see much of . . . the Son.

And there is more. In addition to fighting with visual stimuli, we battle with audio noise—a racket really. And the bombardment of auditory stimuli in our current cultural situation places temptations before us at the rate of hundreds, or even thousands of temptations, per day. I'll have a lot more to say about this later in the book, but it is the unrelenting stimuli of our visual and auditory world that makes the historic Christian practices of silence and solitude such key strategies to save and deliver us from the tyranny of our desires. In solitude and silence you will hear the melodic voice of heaven. You'll soon discover that the sounds of paradise sound much different from what's available on iTunes. Once you can hear the difference, your ability to discern temptation and to find ways out of tempting situations will soar.

The spiritually clarifying and enriching tunes of heaven will become to you a periscope, cranking up from the deep sin pit in which we often live. Breaking the surface of the earth, the lens enables us to see again the Son and make a new path to him.

But what I want you to grasp here is that *much of the noise of life in this world conspires against such clarity*. Most of the loudest messages entering our ears and eyes encourage self-satisfaction. You can now see why Satan and all his minions work so hard to keep us from the ancient fountains of grace found in silence, solitude, Sabbath, and fasting. These four ancient practices and others like them have been used for generations for a reason: they clarify, bringing into focus that which is most real. They expose the destructive lies we errantly believe and reveal the saving, healing truth of God.

We will come back to the role of spiritual disciplines in the later chapters. For now it is enough to recognize that our desires are the core problem when it comes to temptation and that giving into our desires only worsens our plight. Satan knows this and conspires to keep us embattled on all fronts, poking and stoking our desires in his effort to get us to fall.

The Tyranny of Whatever It Takes

A further problem with uncontrolled desire is that when we will *do anything, whatever it takes*, to fulfill a desire, we multiply sin. We harm those around us in pursuit of what we want. Our moment-by-moment, weekly, and monthly disappointments generate an unpleasant temper, a bad mood that then gets worked out on all those around us. We inadvertently create and carry around with us a spiritual atmosphere that is toxic to our loved ones.

I know we live in a sound-bite, web-abbreviated, anti-intellectual world, but the way we think about the subject of temptation actually matters a great deal. A generation ago, C. S. Lewis wrote *The Screwtape Letters*. Using creative conversation between a master devil and his apprentice and cutting to the heart of how temptation works, his book became a Christian classic. In one conversation Screwtape reminds his trainee: "Non-sense in the intellect reinforces corruption in the will."[13] There is no important aspect of human life in which good thinking should not be preferred and valued above poor, wrong, or misguided thinking. The darker our thoughts, the less clarity we have about anything. It is like driving at sunset and forgetting to remove your sunglasses. At some point you realize you are not seeing well, so you remove the sunglasses and enter the world of improved light and sight. Or if you don't live in a locale in which sunglasses are common, think about how much better you can see the night stars when you shift your vantage point from city lights to a completely dark desert or beach. This happened for me when I moved from lit-up Southern California to a small town in Idaho: suddenly I could see what was always there—really bright stars.

This same progress is possible with moral issues, with our inner structure of desire and the temptations they cause. It is the job of this book to show you how to make such moral progress. How can we recover sight? How do we acquire more light? Jesus said he was the light of the world (John 8:12; 9:5). In terms of the essential content of his message, the light to which Jesus points is the polar opposite of the tyranny of our desires. It is a life of total and divine freedom within the kingdom of God. Ongoing and increased knowledge of God and his kingdom agenda can—and I believe *will*—shape your thoughts, your heart, your desires, and your will, and then your behavior.

Ancient and Fruitful Practice

Mull over this prayer for a while; stay with it until you feel in your deepest being that these words, spoken on behalf of God by ministers all over the globe, are true about you.

> *Almighty God have mercy on you, forgive you all your sins through our Lord Jesus Christ, strengthen you in all goodness, and by the power of the Holy Spirit keep you in eternal life.* Amen.[14]

THREE

THE INSIDER
REPORT

The heart of a man is revealed in temptation ...
for in temptation man knows on what
he has set his heart.
—DIETRICH BONHOEFFER[1]

Because temptations are often rooted in something created by God as "good," they always look appealing. They coax, induce, allure, and seduce us. *Temptation*, in the typical use of the term, suggests an act, word, or attitude that brings negative consequences if acted upon. For most of us, if we are merely playing a simple game of word association, *temptation* also calls to mind a lack of self-control. None of us likes to admit that we cannot control ourselves in the face of temptation.

More to the point, we don't completely *want* to control ourselves. After all, temptation can be exciting. It can stimulate obsessive desire and passionate feelings. It is both sobering and sad that today many people feel most alive, most human, most *them* when they experience the adrenaline rush of temptation.

Thus some people actually put themselves in the position to be tempted on purpose. It is fun to them. It's entertainment. It takes the focus off the hard things of life for a few pleasurable moments. So these people actually cultivate wrong desire for fear that they would otherwise be cut off from that which makes them feel most alive. Such a state of things is what leads to the boa constrictor effect I described in the previous chapter. It doesn't start with a death choke, however. It starts with a thought.

Every Thought Captive

To have a thought is not a sin. To have something flit across your mind is not wrong. This is not the same as saying that you cannot sin with your mind or your thoughts, for surely you can. You can sin with your thoughts by *flirting* with what *flits*, by dwelling lustfully upon that which enters your mind. But the thought alone is not sin. This truth is very important and offers powerful deliverance from unnecessary guilt and shame. How about this? Maybe God is proud of you when, having had a thought cross your mind, you chose to ignore it for the sake of the greater good of loving God and neighbor.

The apostle Paul said that he strove to "take captive every thought to make it obedient to Christ" (2 Corinthians 10:5). A section of the *The Message* from 2 Corinthians 10 gives us the context and powerful motive of Paul. It also alerts us to why many of us are helpless when confronted by tempting thoughts. Read it and see if you can find the source of defeat.

> We use our powerful God-tools for smashing warped phi-losophies, tearing down barriers erected against the truth of God, fitting every loose thought and emotion and impulse into the structure of life shaped by Christ. Our tools are ready at hand for clearing the ground of every obstruction and building lives of obedience into maturity.

Did you see it? Many of us deal poorly with sin because we simply do not have Paul's worldview and the aspirations and goals that spring from it. Look at the text again. Paul was up to something. He was headed somewhere. He was follow-ing Jesus and trying to make sense of life on that basis. This is what is referred to by these words: "We are . . . fitting every loose thought and emotion and impulse into *the structure of a life shaped by Christ . . . and building lives of obedience into maturity*" (emphasis added).

I want us now to consider a hugely important question. The answer to this question will predict how well you will do with temptation in the future and how serious you are about battling temptation now. It's also the explanation for how well you have been doing in the past. This question is of paramount importance because, as James K. A. Smith notes, the question implies something at the heart of humanity: "we are defined by . . . and made distinctive by what we love . . ."[2] Furthermore, Smith helps us see the truth that "we are fun-damentally desiring creatures . . . pulled [into action] by what we desire."[3] Just before you see the big question, note this truism from Smith: ". . . we cannot *not* be lovers; we can't *not* be desiring some kingdom. The question is not *whether* we will love but *what* we love"[4] (emphasis his).

Here's the question: *Around what or whom are you seeking to structure your life?*

Spiritually speaking, that is a billion-dollar question. It is the only possible gauge by which one can know what to do with thoughts, feelings, impulses, inclinations, and drives. What makes the question so important is simply this: If temptations are rooted in things that God created good, but our disordered desires are the principal problem, how do we rightly order them so that we do not distort what God created good? If you are shooting for a life shaped by Christ and building a life of obedience into Jesus-loving and others-loving maturity, that intention, that commitment alone, will set aside and screen out the vast majority of sinful thoughts and feelings that come your way. Without such a commitment? Well, keep your eye out for boa constrictors on the way to your next buy, fix, or encounter.

Why Bother?

Those of us who regularly give in to temptation do so for less than a handful of simple reasons:

- We don't know what *success* looks like—we have no vision for victory over temptation.
- We don't *intend* to succeed.

- We don't know *how or where* to begin.
- We therefore have no *strategy* for success.

The lack of vision or desire to succeed, the nonintentionality that comes from it, the lack of insight about where to begin, and the absence of a strategy are usually accompanied by these common feelings, thoughts, and attitudes:

- **Hopelessness**: I've given up; I've tried and failed too many times.
- **Guilt**: I'm overwhelmed by my failures, offenses, and wrongdoings.
- **Fear of failure**: I am scared to try, frightened by what failure may mean.
- **Avoidance of hypocrisy**: If I don't make any public attempts, if I "keep it real," I cannot be criticized when I inevitably fail.
- **Lack of energy to fight**: The temptation must just be *me*; I need to relax, stop the fight, and accept *me* by accepting the temptation.

Think about the last time you faced a temptation of some kind. Did you do anything specific to avoid giving in to the temptation? We polled Americans on that same question. What we heard back comprises, for me, one of the most noteworthy findings of the study: apparently 59 percent[5] of all Americans said, "No, I did not do anything specific to avoid the temptation." For younger people, roughly college age, the number was even higher: 65 percent.[6] The picture is a bit brighter when the question is asked of those who practice the Christian faith. Only 36 percent of Protestants said they do nothing, while 49 percent of Catholics said the same.

Regarding avoiding temptation, it looks like the majority of Americans say, "Why bother?" and sizable minorities of Christians do the same. These stats may sound far-fetched. They may cause us to wonder, can anyone really live that way? The cynical among us may simply say, "That explains Vegas and certain websites!" But I think I get it: if you've got no compelling reason to do so, why would you bother battling temptation?

It's not the lack of effort that should stun us. It is the lack of a story that shapes one's life, a story that is capable of producing a moral imagination leading to moral effort.

Let's now look into the dirty little secret of what motivates temptation in Americans.

Why We Are Tempted

In addition to helping the people cited above who "do nothing specific" to avoid temptation, there is a second compelling rationale for this book to be written: *50 percent of Americans are not sure why they give into temptation*. That's like saying 50 percent of the people thrown into the pool of life can't swim. Or that 50 percent of the people on the road of life can't drive. Those of us in greater Los Angeles already know that, but you get my larger point: half of us have no hope of overcoming temptation. We do not even understand the process of giving in!

In my work as a pastor, professor, and leader of various kinds of organizations, I have heard more times than I can remember: "I don't know why I do what I do!" This comment is usually loaded with hopelessness and shame. The next part of this chapter could do Americans a lot of good if it achieves the modest goal of exposing the inner workings of temptation so that no one any longer has to be in the position of despairing self-unawareness.

The top reason 20 percent of Americans identify for falling into sin is to *escape or get away from real life for a while.* Are there five people who regularly sit around your dinner table or sit with you at lunch? In most cases one of you is trying to avoid your real, actual life by creating an alternative life by yielding to temptation. In various spiritual conversations, I have heard this explained: "No one knows how hard my life is. I simply cannot make it on my own. I need some relief, some comfort. How bad can it [any particular vice] be if it is helping me hang on as a spouse, parent, or student?"

The next statistically relevant reason Americans give for falling into temptation is to *feel less pain or loneliness.* Only 8 percent cited that as the main reason for giving in to temptation, but I'd bet this explains some of the 50 percent of Americans who are not conscious of why they give in to temptation. I've heard students, parishioners, and coworkers confess the need to feel less pain by comments such as, "I needed to find a way to cope. The pain of divorce [or job loss, the death of a loved one, or some other challenge] was more than I could bear. I was just looking for something to knock the edge off so I could at least function on a minimal level."

The last notable reason for giving in to temptation, provided by 7 percent of Americans, is to *satisfy people's expectations of us*. I can't know for sure, but again my experienced guess would be that if Americans were more aware of the cognitive and emotional processes within them, "people's expectations" would account for some of the unexplained 50 percent mentioned above. Here is a common pattern I've often heard to express a person's interactions with others' expectations: "He has some sort of unexplained power over me. I promise myself I won't give in, but I always do. I then feel horrible about it and make the same promise yet again. But then I get around him and I just can't help myself!"

Let's pause for a moment here and circle back to our earlier work, our crucial insight about dealing with temptation by *reordering our disordered system of desire*. Reading further into the data, can you now see how it works? *Getting away from life for a bit* is simply a normal, average, standard, and ordinary rationalization for a disordered desire. That last sentence may cause you to ask, what does the rightly ordered system of desire look like? It has these driving thoughts: *I don't have to have what I want or think I need. "The Lord is my shepherd I shall not be in want"* (Psalm 23:1 NLT).

Feeling less pain is rooted in, and is made sense of in, a life story that does not include suffering as a way to grow in Christian spirituality. The practice of avoiding pain at all costs is a failure to understand and believe that we are always safe in the kingdom of God—no matter what the circumstances. This *no pain* mind-set forgets that sometimes God speaks best in our longings and pain.

Satisfying others' expectations grows from the disordered soil of not rooting our identity in God, in his story, and in his people.

I know I have oversimplified a bit in the last couple of paragraphs; pain is a worthy topic for a whole other book. Here my intention is to simply alert you that once we start down paths of sin, rationalized by strong (but disordered) desire, our lives will become even more misshapen. The more conscious you can become of this common process, the better you will be able to see temptation for what it is: a sign of where you already stand, the true arrangement of your existing system of desire. There is a spiral here, a death dive, a moral gravity and suction that pulls us down with it. Happily, on the other hand, reorienting our desires, changing our inner stance and position, also has a strong pull of its own, naturally producing increasing levels of righteousness as a tree, in accordance with its inner nature, naturally bears fruit.

Let's look now at the strategies of the 41 percent[7] of Americans who do try to avoid temptation.

Avoiding Temptation

When pressed to reveal their hearts, here is what Americans say they do to avoid temptation:[8]

1. Pray, asking God for help or strength.
   That's good news, huh? Clarifications given to us in the survey included: "I count on my religious faith when tempted." "I remind myself of my core values

41

and faith." "I pray . . . quote Bible verses . . . and ask God to help and guide me."

2. Use reason and reminders, convince myself, weigh options.
   Typically cited comments were: "I calm myself down before I can say or do something wrong." "I used a designated driver to avoid the temptation to drive drunk."

3. Just say no and choose not to participate.
   This is the will or volition in action. Interesting explanations were: "Instead of eating, I put it off for fifteen minutes and usually get over the desire." "I was very tempted to have an affair, but I stopped talking to the person that made me feel that way."

4. Avoid the source of temptation; stay away from it.
   This is similar to number 3 above, but the related comments are enlightening: "I deleted a pornographic e-mail from my friend before viewing it." "I was very depressed and wanted a drink. But I am trying to quit drinking so I gave my credit and debit cards to my partner to hold on to so I wouldn't be able to purchase anything until the craving passed."

5. Leave the scene of temptation, get away, go home.
   Are you seeing a theme begin to emerge? Yet again

the commentary is instructive: "Flee! As in completely avoid or change the environment of temptation." "Get out of the kitchen!" "Remove myself completely and immediately from the situation."

6. Substitute other activities, focus on something else, change the subject.
   The theme of avoidance continues with these comments: "I put my mind on something else." "I try to think of role models—what would they think if they saw me?"

7. Consider the outcome, consequences, and effects.
   Representative comments were: "I think of my husband and what he would think of me if I gave in." "I think of my whole household: what would they lose if I gave in?"

8. Talk to others, to self; talk myself out of the temptation.
   The typical remarks that came back on the survey were: "I talk to a friend." "I talk to my spouse." "I try to talk to myself to convince myself not to give in."

9. Exercise or engage in physical activity.
   The testimonies along these lines were: "I go for a walk instead of engaging with the temptation." Many people said, "I go for a walk, listen to music, and meditate." Or, "I keep myself busy with exercise."

10. Take preventive measures.

Several avoidance mechanisms tied for tenth place. I chose this one because among the four that tied, this is the most enlightening. Here are a couple of typical remarks: "I get busy with my grandchildren." "I keep myself busy with hobbies or crafts."

Glance quickly back at the tactics and behaviors in the list above. I notice a pattern: almost all of them are outward and temporary. I don't mean to say that this is completely wrong-headed. For instance, if a hooligan were tempted to break into my car to steal my phone, I would be very happy if he refrained, even for one of the less-than-great reasons above. But, while happy for me, I would still be concerned about the person walking away with his wrong desires still intact.

The criticism of the not-so-good methods above isn't that they don't work sometimes for some people. The criticism is this: many of them (use of a designated driver, avoidance, substitutions, keeping busy, and so on) are outward, mechanical, and short-term. The better way, the Jesus Way, is inward, transformational, and long-term.

Some respondents to the Barna survey get near to the Jesus Way and may, in fact, be there. God and prayer top the list. Eighteen percent of all adults who try something to avoid temptation turn to God in prayer. But there is an interesting age discrepancy at play in prayer: only 3 percent[9] of the youngest group in the study say they have God as their first and primary point of reference and are talking to him about their temptations. On the other end of the age spectrum, 33 percent of elders, those sixty-five and older, say they turn first to God.[10]

Besides noting this interesting religious demographic, we should also note something more important in these two stats: the loss of the biblical story as *the* story for our lives. Older people, in my experience, tend to have maintained a biblical context for their lives and their various choices. Young people, on the other hand, do not for the most part know the basic Christian story of the Bible. Thus they often lack an instinctual, biblically based reason for making better moral choices or refraining from negative behaviors. But they also lack something more important: the knowledge that there is a personal God to whom they can relate. This distinctly Christian view of the world is almost entirely debunked among their peers. Without the knowledge of a personal God, why would one pray? The best option one is left with is what the youngest among us do: think one's best thoughts and make one's best moral decisions within a relativistic worldview of "whatever!" If one thinks there is no God or that there is a God but he does not have any interaction with the goings-on and people of earth, then one is not apt to have a conversational relationship with the god so conceived.

All that is left is what young people, who if they do anything at all, say they use to deal with temptation: reason, self-will, and various avoidance mechanisms.[11] I'll say more below, but whatever effectiveness there is in these approaches—and there is some—is short-lived, and these approaches cannot produce long-standing change in the inner structure of disordered desire. It is like amputating a leg to deal with a virus or bacteria: it is better than nothing, but it may not deal with the whole, hidden disease circulating in the body parts that remain after the amputation.

I highlight young people here because the survey shows that they are much more inclined than forty-six- to sixty-five-year-olds to worry, procrastinate, overuse media, be lazy, spend too much money, gossip, envy, use porn, or cheat.[12] This observation shouts the question, why?

In times past, the conventional wisdom has been that "life teaches us," that the "school of moral hard knocks bangs us into moral shape." But what if a new reality is in play today? What if the process that was assumed over the last few decades cannot be assumed, at least not in the same way and with the same amount of confidence?

For instance, what if kids won't come back to church when they finish college, marry, or have children as previous generations did? What if young people are tempted more because society, having lost its moral compass, is not helping them in the way that society, with its behavioral norms, once kept their parents and grandparents in check? Young people certainly have more ways to access sin than any generation in the history of mankind.

Whatever the underlying causes of the survey, the numbers speak loudly. But they do not merely reveal a negative trend with young people; for me, particularly as a pastor and father, they reveal hope. Young people may be more tempted, but they are also, when they can see a new path, more courageous and more adventuresome in going down it. Where they may lack moral clarity, they can make up for it with moral energy if they can see the right way to go.

Thus the observations above are not meant to criticize young people. I am actually optimistic about them. They may be confused about God, but they are working hard to make sense of their techno-global-wired world that no one has ever before inhabited. They will end up shaping this new world. They know this, even if subconsciously. As I describe life with Jesus in the classroom and in casual conversations, the only hostility I find is toward stereotypes of Christians and Christianity that all of us would reject. I find huge openness to hearing about Jesus, about God's plan to restore creation, about life in the kingdom as a student of Jesus. Young people are open to finding new ways of making the world and their inner world work—including God's ways.

The Jesus Way

The church, with few exceptions because of its low standing among young people, does not have much of a counteracting voice in the discussion regarding the "no god" or "distant god" view that is often taught to young Americans in schools and on the street. But Jesus, if not his church, still has some standing in the culture among all age groups. If you are a young reader, pay special attention to the words of Jesus in the next few paragraphs. If you are older and have loving concern for a child or grandchild, the thoughts that follow will give hope and enlighten you too.

Let's begin by working with the positive instinct of the people in the Barna study who commented, "I pray," "I talk to myself," and so on. These are glimpses of a turn inward, where the real battle of temptation is fought. This is the genius of the Jesus Way. Jesus said:

> A good tree cannot bear bad fruit, and a bad tree cannot bear good fruit. (Matthew 7:18)

> Woe to you, teachers of the law and Pharisees, you hypocrites! You clean the outside of the cup and dish, but inside they are full of greed and self-indulgence. Blind Pharisee! First clean the inside of the cup and dish, and then the outside also will be clean. Woe to you, teachers of the law and Pharisees, you hypocrites! You are like whitewashed tombs, which look beautiful on the outside but on the inside are full of the bones of the dead and everything unclean. (Matthew 23:25–27)

Those words of Jesus may not sound encouraging on the surface, but look deeper. Jesus is calling our attention to two things. One, an outward approach to dealing with temptation does not, and cannot, work. As we have been stressing up to this point, the real battle with temptation is not the stimuli that are external to us but a fallen, damaged structure of desire within us. Two, if we are to change what we do with our bodies, the visible parts we use to sin, we must change the inner reality that controls the parts.

This is Jesus' point regarding trees: they produce visible fruit based on invisible DNA within them. It cannot be otherwise with trees and their fruit. With these shrewd words, Jesus invites us to examine the inner DNA of our desires. What are they, really? Where did they come from? Are you stuck with them forever? Would you like to reorder them?

Jesus' insight concerning dishes and tombs leads in the same brilliant direction: When it comes to spiritual growth, when it comes to reordering the hidden desires that lead us into temptation, we must turn inward to make an outward difference. Cleaning the inside of the cup will lead to the outside being clean as a by-product. Cleaning the outside of a tomb, a respectful thing to do, leaves the inward death in place. New life comes only from going inward, to our *heart*, as Jesus said, the interior place from where our words and deeds come (Matthew 12:34; 15:8, 18–19).

As we move into the next chapter, we will discover the process of temptation and how to have substantial victory over it using the insights of Jesus. I say *substantial* because *perfection* can never be in view. Inserting perfection into the conversation brings two decidedly unhelpful things to bear: a reason to not try at all, or alternatively, shame. Shame is utterly unhelpful because it kills momentum. Let's keep clear of perfection and head instead for steady progress in the right direction. If you are in the grip of temptation, you did not get there overnight. Be patient, give yourself some space, and operate in peace. It may take some time to reorder out-of-control desire.

Having seen the stats, stories, and rationales for contemporary temptations, it is time to look more deeply into our favorite sins. Not to understand the sins, but to understand the underlying system of desire from which they come. And not just to understand desire as a philosophical or moral concept, but to find a new heart and new practices that are rooted in love and loyalty to God and his purposes for the church.

Remember my comments from chapter 1: you may not see yourself exactly in the five stories that follow. But by now you should know this is okay. It is the underground root—disordered desire—that is the same in all of us, not the particular flower that may sway in the air. The following stories—revealing hearts, baring the truth of inner battles, and describing the context in which the struggle occurs—will give you more of what you need to battle temptation, whatever your particular temptation may be.

Anxious Annie will get us headed in that direction.

Ancient and Fruitful Practice

Contemplate the prayer below, reading it slowly and briefly pausing on all the words that strike you as important today. Then choose one word on which to base a prayer for deliverance from the temptation you struggle with most.

> *Almighty God, you alone can bring into order the unruly wills and affections of sinners: Grant your people grace to love what you command and desire what you promise; that, among the swift and varied changes of the world, our hearts may surely there be fixed where true joys are to be found; through Jesus Christ our Lord, who lives and reigns with you and the Holy Spirit, one God, now and for ever.* Amen.[13]

FOUR

ANXIOUS ANNIE

Good thoughts bear good fruit, bad thoughts bear bad fruit—and man is his own gardener.
—DIETRICH BONHOEFFER[1]

"I hate to admit it," Annie told me, "but my earliest memory is of worry." She continued:

In the recollection I am about five to six years old, sitting on the edge of my bed, early on a Saturday morning, socked feet dangling down just above the carpet. That was my favorite place and posture for anxiety. In this case I was worrying about my cat. The night before Mom had told me that our cat, being fourteen years old, could soon be going to cat heaven. I had fallen asleep surprisingly well after talking to

Mom, but something got into my head during the night because I did not just wake up that morning, I shot up as if cold water had been splashed in my face, the way one might wake to thunder in Florida or an earthquake in California.

I think this was tough news because actually the family cat was my cat. Freddie spent all his time in my room curled up on a pillow at the foot of my bed. Plus, while it scared me, I had no real idea what Mom meant. I could not have passed a test on "dead" or "heaven," if you know what I mean. I could feel her love and care for me in her warning about Freddie. But thinking about this over the past couple of sessions with my counselor, I now know I also could sense some anxiety in her tone of voice and body language. And what did "dead" mean? What does a dead cat look like? What is heaven? I'd heard talk of it around the house and in Sunday school, but I had no clear picture in my mind of either reality. Nonetheless, that weekend I met my mortal enemy—worry.

For as long as I can remember, worry, fear, and anxiety have been my companions during the normal transitions and challenges of life. At times I feel paralyzed, cut off from life, afraid to think about what is out there. I'm even afraid of what my life might look like if I weren't anxious—how crazy is that! But I'm also afraid of staying as I am and never really living my life.[2]

I've tried everything I can think of to overcome

worry. My counselor asked me one day for a list of the coping mechanisms I have used to deal with my anxiety. After she explained to me what a "coping mechanism" was (handling my stress in indirect ways), I went home and produced this list for my next appointment:

- *I try to calm myself down before I say or do something wrong.*
- *I try to remind myself of my core values and faith.*
- *I try to leave anxious environments.*
- *I try to think positive thoughts . . . and just say no to anxious thoughts and feelings.*
- *I talk to my two best friends about the way I am feeling and acting.*[3]

I haven't had the nerve to tell my counselor yet that my nightly wine consumption has grown to the very top of the largest glass I can find in the cupboard. But I was honest about the other things. And most of the time those things do help. But I've come to realize that the fix is only temporary. My worry is like water in a toilet: I can flush it down, but it comes right back, filling the bowl to the level where it was before I pressed the handle.

Wearied by Worry

Annie's story is, in part, like the kind of story we see on television crime shows: "these are fictional stories; they do not represent any particular person." Annie is a composite of people I've known, and in that sense she is fictional. But she is indeed representative of millions of Americans. When we polled Americans, the Annies of America came out on top. According to Barna, 60 percent[4] of Americans say they are often or sometimes tempted to worry or to be drawn by life into anxiety. This is not surprising. Most of us know family or friends who are on antianxiety meds, whether smoked or in pills from a bottle, prescribed or bought on the street.

Some will doubtless wonder if anxiety is even a sin. "I thought it was a nervous disorder," they'll say. "It is not possible to live without worry!" I know this is not intuitive for many people, but anxiety, worry, and fear are undoubtedly sins at certain excessive levels. They miss the mark of God's intention for humans. They distance us from God. Even if unspoken or unconscious, they doubt God's power or goodness. I believe it is the feeling of doubting God and the accompanying distancing from him that cause 60 percent of Americans to list anxiety as their top temptation. Now the complexity and pace of modern life, with all its blazing-fast changes, make occasional low-level anxiety normal and inevitable. But when anxiety rises to the level of causing us to doubt the person and power of God, then it is sinful. This kind of worry-anxiety does no good. We are immobilized by it. It thwarts our formation into Christlikeness.

Recognizing anxiety as a less-than-ideal spiritual state is certainly a part of the biblical tradition:

- Solomon said, "What do people get for all the toil and anxious striving with which they labor under the sun? All their days their work is grief and pain; even at night their minds do not rest. This too is meaningless" (Ecclesiastes 2:22–23).

- Jesus said, "I tell you not to worry about your life. Don't worry about having something to eat, drink, or wear" (Matthew 6:25 CEV).
- Paul said, "Do not be anxious about anything" (Philippians 4:6).

Invitations to a state of peace are also prevalent:

- "When I said, 'My foot is slipping,' your unfailing love, LORD, supported me. When anxiety was great within me, your consolation brought me joy" (Psalm 94:18–19).
- "Live carefree before God; he is most careful with you" (1 Peter 5:7 MSG).
- Jesus said, "Peace I leave with you; my peace I give you. I do not give to you as the world gives. Do not let your hearts be troubled and do not be afraid" (John 14:27).

Despite what many of us know from the Bible, anxiety is a real problem. More than half of Americans are so in touch with its effect on their lives that it is the first thing that comes to their minds when questioned about what tempts them. I don't think respondents answered the question based on a thorough knowledge of the debates among psychologists and theologians regarding how anxiety works and which elements of it are sin versus "just life." I think they were noting the sores in their mouths, their racing hearts, their chronic fatigue and sore muscles and bones, their short tempers, and their inability to sleep. Either way, it is an epidemic among us, as any teacher, counselor, pastor, parent, or spouse can tell you.

Transformational Information

I love being in the classroom, whether learning or teaching, and I do not mean to knock truth, good thinking, or intelligence when I say what I am about to say. But preachy advice does not often help people deal with temptation. We greatly overestimate the value of mere information to bring about change. In fact, as N. T. Wright says, "To tell someone not to yield to a particular temptation merely puts the idea of it into their minds, to be handled and fondled with interest and perhaps delight."[5]

I've misunderstood this for much of my life, both as a parent and as an employer and boss. When presented with a problem, my first instinct is too often to learn my way into it and teach my way out of it. I often feel that if I can shine the light of knowledge on something, I can create or facilitate behavior change. When my son started dabbling in harmful stuff, I tried to reason with him and tell him that I had tried it all and that I could assure him that there was nothing there. When coworkers will not pick up a task I give them, I always assume they need to know more. But often what I need to do is pay attention to how they are feeling and what position they are in.

Information alone does not produce change because it does not touch the will, the emotions, the heart, the spirit, or our social environment. These things have to work with knowledge in a deep and profound synergy if knowledge is going to produce victory over temptation. Many approaches to Christian discipleship, rooted in bits of Bible knowledge but lacking interaction with our heart, will, emotions, and desires are "like pouring water on our head to put out a fire in our heart."[6]

For instance, if I say two plus two is four or that France is a country in Europe, a certain kind of truth, enlightenment, or revelation takes place. But switch gears with me here for a moment. I am about five feet eleven inches tall. Why should you care about that piece of data? Because of what I am about to say now: in the early 1990s I weighed about 330 pounds! I was seriously obese. When I see the pictures, though I of course remember the events and scenes from which the photos come, I am stunned by what I see: the enormity of me!

If someone had said something perfectly true, accurate, and even loving to me like, "Todd, you are getting really . . . large . . . uh . . . big . . . really fat," that bit of information would not have sparked change in me. I probably would have replied with some kind of sarcastic humor like, "No kidding! I hadn't noticed. I thought my belt was the equator!" Lots of kind and loving friends or family members said true, accurate, and helpful things to me during my season of immenseness. But information on that level is not transformational. I needed something that would reorder my desire away from excessive food. Now, that was information I could have used. But where could I go to find such insight?

This thought from N. T. Wright certainly could have helped me at the time:

> The answer to temptation is to find out, perhaps over a long period, what it is about you that is at the moment out of shape, distorted, in pain. Then one may begin to find out, often painfully, how it is that God longs to help you to get what is distorted back into focus; to get what is crooked back into shape; to get what is bruised and hurt back into health.[7]

But these things—pain, distortion, and misshapenness—are all deep and profound things, usually buried in places we think we can never discover. To me it felt like the times you hide something in a safe place, and then, outsmarting yourself and not the bad guys, you forget where you put it. How do we get at these subterranean, multilayered things? What do we do to cooperate with the loving God-longing that Wright describes? I'll have a lot to say about this in later chapters, but for now, thinking especially of the 60 percent of us given to worrying too much, focus on this thought from Jesus:

> If God gives such attention to the appearance of wildflowers—most of which are never even seen—don't you think he'll attend to you, take pride in you, do his best for you? What I'm trying to do here is to get you to *relax*, to not be so preoccupied with getting, so you can respond to God's giving. People who don't know God and the way he works

fuss over these things, but you know both God and how he works. Steep your life in God-reality, God-initiative, God-provisions. Don't worry about missing out. You'll find all your everyday human concerns will be met. (Matthew 6 MSG, emphasis added)

I tried to alert you in the earlier chapters to the core pattern for dealing with temptation: deal with your desires— the inner life of thoughts, feelings, will, and heart. Can you hear Jesus guiding us in that direction? *Steep your life in God-reality, God-initiative, God-provisions.* When that happens, when we know in our deep inner *knowers* that, as the psalmist said, "the Lord is my Shepherd" and that we can therefore "wait on the Lord" (Psalm 23, 27), we then enter a new worry-free reality that stops the temptation of anxiety. When we know and *act in faith* on that deep knowledge, our experience of God's provision and care in time grows more real than our cares.

Sin Desires to Have You

Our problem is not merely that we desire to sin; it's that sin desires to have us. It's crouching at the door for us like it did for Cain. Thus we must rule over it (Genesis 4:7). How do we do that? Did God really mean that we could find a way to rule over sin? Yes. How successful are you? Not as much as you would hope, I imagine. That's okay. Perfection is never in view when we speak about success or victory over our temptations. The first letter of John makes this clear:

If we claim to be without sin, we deceive ourselves and the truth is not in us. If we confess our sins, he is faithful and just and will forgive us our sins and purify us from all unrighteousness. (1 John 1:8–9)

My dear children, I write this to you so that you will not sin. But if anybody does sin, we have an advocate with the Father—Jesus Christ, the Righteous One. (1 John 2:1)

John is making a case against sin as a lifestyle. He is saying that new life in Jesus crowds out ongoing, unrepentant sin. But he knows we will not reach perfection, that while sin as habit will fall off, moments of sin will remain. He assures us that these moments of sin—past, present, and future—are completely covered by the death of Jesus, our advocate before the Father. Looking for perfection will only make us crazy. Shooting for perfection often makes us worse kinds of people. But that does not mean we cannot make serious and sustained progress in the spiritual life. We *can* get to the place where we are not ruled by sin, where it's not a habit that defines our lives.

What is the key to progress regarding temptation? The key is understanding how the cosmic game of temptation is played. It is played by the rules of, and on the field of, desire. A scholarly dictionary on ethics makes this clear: "While Satan may attempt to confuse us at the intellectual level with heresy, half-truths and ideological distortions, he also (and often more *fatally*), seeks to manipulate us at more hidden levels of our being; the levels of desire, impulse, instinct, prejudice and fear."[8] Jesus said:

> What comes out of a person is what defiles them. For it is from within, out of a person's heart, that evil thoughts come—sexual immorality, theft, murder, adultery, greed, malice, deceit, lewdness, envy, slander, arrogance and folly. All these evils come from inside and defile a person. (Mark 7:20–23)

Bottom line: either we learn to *have* our desires, or they will *have* us. Deal with angry thoughts, or malice and murder may have you. Deal with lustful thoughts and feelings, or immorality, adultery, and lewdness will have you.

But desires cannot be simply plucked from your soul the way you pull an unsightly weed from a flower bed. Desires just *are*. As I've said, but must repeat here, most desires are rooted in something good or at least represent something that is good. How much worry and anxiety is just a distorted desire for safety, an obvious good? How much lust and lewdness is rooted in a desire for intimacy?

We cannot remove these desires or spray them with spiritual weed killer. These desires are part of us, and like all of us they must be reshaped into the image of Christ as we grow in grace. Those desires that cannot be reshaped must be replaced by different, more Christlike desires, supplanted and superseded by stronger desires for God, his work, and his people. To successfully defeat temptation, we must reorder our desires and become the kind of person who, having feasted on God, his desires and purposes for us, would not entertain temptation.

I Object!

At this point I can hear in my head a couple of points of pushback.

"Wait a minute," you may be asking, "doesn't messing with my structure or system of desires set *me* aside?" No. Resisting temptation does not set *you* aside. Resisting temptation does not kill the real you. It is deformed desire that devastates personhood and that destroys humanity. There is a new you in the image of God, ready to be born, a you that cannot be reduced to your desires.

Someone else may object: "All this talk of eliminating desire sounds a lot like Buddhism." Please note: I am not talking about *eliminating* desire. Even if we tried, we could not come to the place of *no* desire. Furthermore, we need desire in order to pursue the good. Desire, the impulse toward good and godly things, is a core component of spiritual growth and the defeat of temptation. So hang on to desire with all you've got. Just don't let *wrong desire* overwhelm thoughts of godliness, feelings of love for God and his purposes, and your will to follow Jesus.

If you think about it for a moment, this is straightforward. Parents constantly teach kids not to be ruled by desire but to think of others and to consider family rules and community values. Reordering desires, for instance, just means preventing desire for stuff and things from overwhelming your desire to remain true to your commitments—not to steal from your colleagues and friends, not to lose your integrity, and so on.

The other day a friend asked me how a mutual friend of ours could have been unfaithful to his spouse; the offender didn't seem to be the type to sin in that way. In response I said, "People have forgotten how to suffer, how to do the right thing and to suffer in silence for it. They think that to not act on a desire is wrong, that it's somehow dishonest. They think they have to do it or they are not being true to themselves." This, by the way, explains much of the current debate about human sexuality. If a person feels something strongly enough, it must be natural, it must be okay, and thus the desire must be indulged. That line of thinking will never produce the suffering involved in self-denial. But self-imposed suffering is a real and significant part of the Jesus Way. If it weren't, would Christ have told us to pick up our crosses and follow him?

There is no progress in reordering strong desire for evil that does not include suffering. We all have to learn through death-to-self to distinguish "the good" from "what I want," and to suffer pursuing "the good" until our inner self has been reworked and bent toward godly desires.

You don't have to have what you want! It will not kill you to deprive yourself of it. Try it. Don't look lustfully at someone. Did you die? Tell the truth on your expense account. Did you keel over dead? Of course not. But let's be honest here: we often *feel* as though we will die if we don't express the strong desires within us. I'll bet Annie, whom we met at the beginning of this chapter, has not up to this point in her life been able to imagine life without fretting. She probably cannot imagine *existing* without anxiety. Pushing through that scary feeling, or the feeling that we will die if we don't fulfill our desires, is at the heart of the suffering mentioned above.

Let's get specific. How do we stop the progression from desire to thought to temptation to sin? Using the story of Procrastinating Preston, we will now head in that direction.

Ancient and Fruitful Practice

The *Book of Common Prayer* has within it a set of prayers called the Great Litany. It is a series of petitions usually given by clergy and responded to by the worshippers. As a way to begin to think about reordering the thoughts, feelings, and desires of your heart, I commend this selected petition to you. Sit with it for a few moments. Say it to yourself in silence and then say it aloud. Read it again, and then pray it. Mull it over and see what the Spirit may want to bring to your attention regarding the present stance of your heart.

May it please you to give us hearts to love and worship you, and to keep your commandments with careful attention. We urgently and fervently ask: Hear us, Good Lord.

FIVE

PROCRASTINATING PRESTON

We cannot serve our disordered desires and God too. "Adoration of one feeds contempt for the other."
—MATTHEW 6:24

Those of us in one of the arenas of labor that we call *people work* hear amazing and enlightening stories. Pastors, professors, cops, teachers, counselors, retail clerks, attorneys—anyone working with the stuff of human life knows what it is to be constantly surprised and intrigued by a person's story. This is Preston's story.

> *I knew it. We all know it: Tax Day is April 15 every year. It's not like Easter, which shifts Sundays every year. It's not like daylight saving time, sneaking up on you every spring. How I can miss it most years is a*

mystery to me! But this year at least I feel like I have an excuse.

Tax Day fell right in the middle of my spring break. Because an MBA is needed for the promotion I'm seeking at work, I'd been struggling hard to get my assignments in on time. That is not a rarity for me. In fact it was my finance professor who dubbed me Procrastinating Preston. I never did get an assignment to her on time. Just before spring break, I was also studying lots of hours for midterms—and I have only so many hours in a week! Somehow filing my taxes went out the window of my brain until it was too late. I did file for an extension. But I worry that I'll just put it off until it's due in August.

As you can imagine, I've tried lots of techniques to improve my ability to get things done in a timely manner. I've attended seminars and read books, and because it comes up during performance reviews, I've talked to several kind and encouraging bosses about it.

Over the years I've thought a great deal about the consequences of my procrastination. But I can't even scare myself into consistent on-time performance. My scare tactics work only a few weeks and then the fear wears off and the comfort of doing what I want, when I want to do it, returns. I've even appealed to my conscience. I've tried guilt and shame. I tell myself, to no avail, that sometimes my tardiness is flat immoral. I've tried to use my larger goals as a way to keep me motivated.

I feel stuck in the worst way. My friends who are

tempted by chocolate or nasty magazines can just put their mind on something else or avoid the candy and magazine racks at the store. My problem is that I cannot direct my thoughts in any productive way. I would ask God to help me get going in the right direction, but I'd feel like a big hypocrite, so I don't try that.

I guess if I am honest, I feel completely overwhelmed. I can't seem to do life right! And I hear my mother's voice reminding me of it over and over again. No matter what I did, no matter how hard I tried to do things right, it wasn't enough. So now I wonder, why try?

Here's the problem: My resistance to trying, my fear of failure, is no longer just keeping me from cleaning my childhood bedroom. It has taken on a life of its own that I can no longer control. It affects my work; my boss is losing confidence in me. My wife is losing respect for me; my kids are picking up my bad habits. But I can't make myself change.[1]

The Forces of Temptation

Preston is clearly out of control in an important aspect of his life. He is in the grip of powers that he cannot name or neutralize. According to the Barna survey, 60 percent[2] of Americans are in the same state of affairs—they do not understand what is happening to them regarding temptation. What *are* the forces that play upon us when we are in the heat of temptation?

Christian tradition and wisdom boils down the outer battle to two primary enemies: the world and the devil. The *world,* in the sense I use it here, means everything in the world that stands against God: all that is hostile to, and rebellious against, his plans and purposes. The *devil* is a personal spiritual power that leads all the forces of evil that are aligned against God.

These are very simplified definitions, but they are enough for my purpose here: to alert you to a couple of key opponents that work against our formation in Christ. On the inside, or connected to us, we might say, is the *flesh*. Flesh does not mean skin or the fatty tissue below our skin. It does not refer to persons in their material forms. The term *flesh* is not meant to make us hate our bodies—we've got television commercials to do that. Flesh, for our context here, means all aspects of humanity controlled by sinful desires and passions, and thus speaking and acting without any thought of God.

The central battleground of the flesh is the inner life of disordered desire. But desire, as the main battleground, does not exist alone. There are, to continue the military metaphor, the supply-line skirmishes over thoughts and feelings. These two energetic drivers—thoughts and feelings—get pulled into their own side-battles with our will, which is why willpower alone cannot effectively defeat temptation. Your will does not exist in isolation. It is organically joined to the other parts of your being.

To consistently defeat temptation, you must understand what it is that is working on your will from within (thoughts, feelings, memories, and so on) and that which is working against you from the outside (the world and the devil as they play upon your flesh, those parts of you that are misaligned with God). To defeat temptation, you must work to change your *position* relative to inner and outer realities. Let me show you what I mean via a recent experience.

Banging the Button

Recently a cherished friend had what was supposed to be a routine, scheduled, and minor gallbladder surgery. I don't know about you, but I have not believed in *minor* surgery for a long time. Her supposed inconsequential operation quickly turned into what seemed to us in her circle of care to be an episode of *House*.

Because nothing was supposed to go wrong, when it did, there was no little bit of confusion based on the differing opinions of the medical staff. All my friend knew was that she was in serious, debilitating pain, of which no one could find a sure source. Thus she was hooked up to a machine to self-administer pain medication according to the machine-imposed prescription. She was handed something that looked like an early version of a video game controller. It had a red button on top she could push to inject pain medicine directly into her vein.

Being a tough person, she vowed to use it only as absolutely necessary. But as the hours and days wore on and the pain grew increasingly worse, even making breathing hard, she found herself banging the red button as often as the machine would let her. Maybe you've seen a loved one, at the end of a terminal illness, do the same thing. The challenge for my friend was this: the pain medication was never going to work. What was happening inside her body had to be fixed from the inside or the pain was never going away, even under the power of strong drugs.

Regarding temptation, I see people making the exact same mistake and getting the same ineffective results: we bang on the button of our *will*, but the pain of unmet *desire* remains. This is the problem Preston is trying to describe to us. He tried everything to will himself into getting the right thing done at the right time. But as he testified, that approach yielded nothing lasting. There is a reason for this. Our wills are only rarely determinative in the long term. It is not so much that we are weak concerning our will or willpower. It is that other, equally strong influences are always trying to control the will.

These pressures come from, among other things, our thoughts, feelings, and memories. The problem with relying on the will alone is that the will is simply a reflection of the current state of our whole person—the very person that is out of control. Employing the will is not like going to the garage to find a broom to clean up a mess. The will is us; it is how we do what we are currently doing. To see how this works, let's sit with Preston for a bit longer.

Every time Preston tried to will himself into getting a project done on time, he'd be afflicted by the notion that he did not *feel* like working on it just then. Those feelings would then become consistent and normative. He'd then try to ratchet up his will by guilt and shame, only to have the *thought* that "there is always tomorrow." Just then he'd *remember* how good it felt, at least in the moment, to get outside in the fresh air for some golf. No matter how much he banged on his will, his thoughts, memories, and feelings ganged up on his will and regularly defeated it—and him.

Where to now? At this point you may be saying that the only thing you would have known to do was to bang the will button. Good news: there is a wisdom that is available to us all. You do not need to have a high IQ to understand it, and you don't have to be superspiritual to obtain it. It is Proverbial Wisdom. It opens to us a vision for the possibility of spiritual transformation, for changing the desires that seem to have a life of their own within us.

Wisdom Concerning Temptation

Let's work through these concepts from Proverbs in a "problem and solution" manner.

PROBLEM: I have given myself over to my desires so many times that I seem to have abdicated my whole life to them. I seem to have given desire the right to rule over me. When this happens the good feelings of fulfilling my desires dominate me. Getting desires met also dominates my whole mind: "all I can think about is him"; "my every thought seems to be about what I will eat next."

PROVERBIAL SOLUTION (25:28): Self-control of the inner life of desire is the key: "Like a city whose walls are broken through [making the city vulnerable to defeat] is a person who lacks self-control." It is self-control in the areas of thoughts and feelings that rearranges or cuts off desire. Thus self-discipline is a cardinal virtue. But it cannot win alone. It needs the passion of managed feelings and the clarity of good thought to work alongside it. Not to mention the greatest power of all: the love and grace of God.

PROBLEM: I seem so immature about the effects of giving in to temptation. My parents and girlfriend have tried to tell me many times over the past five years, but when the heat is on, probable and future consequences fly away while known and present gratification makes large nests in my mind.

PROVERBIAL SOLUTION (6:27, 28; 22:5; 27:12): "Can a man scoop fire into his lap without his clothes being burned? Can a man walk on hot coals without his feet being scorched? In the paths of the wicked are snares and pitfalls . . . the simple keep going and pay the penalty." The more we get in terms of satisfying sinful desire in the heat of sin—fire and coal—the less or worse of a person we become. We become burned and scorched.

The story of original sin in Genesis is also instructive on this point: "Then the eyes of both of them [Adam and Eve] were opened, and they realized they were naked . . . 'I was afraid . . . so I hid'" (Genesis

3:7–10). Nothing Adam and Eve achieved by giving in to their disordered desire to mistrust God worked for the good: nakedness (in the sense of shame), fear, hiding, and death is what came of it. In Proverbial terms it was all burning, scorching, penalty. Galatians 5 clinches the argument: "It is obvious what kind of life develops out of trying to get your own way all the time: repetitive, loveless, cheap sex; a stinking accumulation of mental and emotional garbage; frenzied and joyless grabs for happiness; trinket gods; magic-show religion; paranoid loneliness; cutthroat competition; all-consuming-yet-never-satisfied wants; a brutal temper; an impotence to love or be loved; divided homes and divided lives; small-minded and lopsided pursuits; the vicious habit of depersonalizing everyone into a rival; uncontrolled and uncontrollable addictions; ugly parodies of community. I could go on" (Galatians 5:19–21 MSG).

PROBLEM: I cannot resist temptation. The enticements toward pleasure are too strong for me. Most of the time I cannot even think of a good reason to resist. It seems to me that there is only one life, so why should I deny myself the things I want—especially when they don't seem to hurt anyone else?

PROVERBIAL SOLUTION (1:10): "My son, if sinful men entice you, do not give in to them." While

I've said that will, willpower, and intention alone are not enough to reliably defeat temptation, you should not therefore think that the will is worthless. The Venerable Bede, a seventh-century monk in England, taught that there are three stages in temptation: "suggestion, experiment and consent."[3]

Based on my experience and observation of others, Bede's pattern holds true. Notice that our God-given will is able to intervene for us at any of the three points. But as we've said, this works best and most consistently when our thoughts, feelings, and social relationships are aligned with our will, which alone is not sufficient to consistently resist temptation.

Desire, Temptation, and Sin

The alignment of our will with our thoughts, feelings, and social relationships can seem like a long way off and a long time coming. Thus many of us have developed coping skills to save us from ourselves in the meantime. Changing our situation and circumstances through coping skills is sometimes a good stopgap, a short-term strategy to stay out of *sin*. But mere coping does not go nearly deep enough. Coping does not get to the level of *temptation* that is rooted in *desire*.

One scholar, commenting on the biblical letter of James, uses this clear idea to explain how temptation works: temptation is only temptation "when it finds an answering chord within us."[4] We tend to locate temptation in the purring voice on the other end of a phone call. In reality the only voice with power to move us to sin is the voice of desire within: the voice calling us to indulge what we think, feel, or observe. It is a wicked voice. This is why spiritual masters like the early church father John Chrysostom said, "I beg you right from the start not to welcome any corrupt thought, for if we do so the seeds will grow inside us, and if we get to that stage, the sin inside us will come out in deeds and strike us dead by condemning us, in spite of all our confessions and tears. For there is nothing more destructive than sin."[5]

The Bent to Consent

Let's pause to review. To be tempted means there is within us a preexisting desire or bent to consent. When that is the case, we are like a cheetah lying in wait for a passing gazelle. When we are living with disordered desires, we are placed and poised in a ready position to pounce on temptation as soon as it presents itself; we may even feel helpless in the face of temptation and believe that we can do nothing different. "Like the cheetah," we say, "there is nothing we can do about our deep human instincts to hunt for sources that fulfill our desires."

But that does not have to be the final verdict. We need Preston, above, to know these hopeful and grounding truths: Our sinful thoughts do not have to, automatically, lead to sinful acts. We do not have to pile up sinful acts that then become sinful habits. We do not have to live with sinful habits that in turn misshape our character. Nothing has the power to tempt me to do wrong action, except I give it that power by what I permit to be alive and well within me: sinful or false thoughts, corrupt feelings, and weak engagements with my will.

Eating Eddie has a few things he can teach us about this.

Ancient and Fruitful Practice

We too often think we can hide the inner battle with desire and temptation. But this prayer, used for five hundred years in nearly every Sunday service in Anglican churches all over the world, reminds us we cannot so hide. Read it once to let it prophesy to you—let it "hurt." Read it a second time to find a vision—let that vision "heal" disordered desire within you.

> *Almighty God, to you all hearts are open, all desires known, and from you no secrets are hid: Cleanse the thoughts of our hearts by the inspiration of your Holy Spirit, that we may perfectly love you, and worthily magnify your holy Name; through Christ our Lord.* Amen.[6]

SIX

EATING EDDIE

SEEKER: *"What must I do to please God?"*

OLD MONK: *"Control your tongue and your stomach."*

—HENRI NOUWEN[1]

For Eddie any strong emotion signaled something deep within him to eat. Every day to celebrate school being over, he wanted his mom to make some fresh flour tortillas, heat them over the fire, and put some butter on them for a snack. If Eddie was worried or sad, he would bug me to walk to the corner store with him to get something sugary to eat, usually a candy bar or soft drink. If we won the ball game in the street, he wondered what we had at our house to eat, maybe some cookies in the cupboard.

When Eddie entered his college years, he often

complained that he felt empty inside, like his emotional and intellectual gas tank was nearly empty. This often led to a trip to a gas station store to buy one of those energy drinks that you see advertised everywhere.

Worst of all, the more Eddie ate, especially the sweet stuff, the worse he felt. It was a terrible cycle to behold: weary, eat; tired, eat; energy-less, eat; worried, eat; stressed, eat. We used to joke that it was a good thing Eddie didn't like alcohol or drugs or the cycle above could have been a lot worse.

An unexpected trip to the doctor's office confirmed what Eddie already knew. He was overweight. The chart on the wall of the doctor's office said "obese." While Eddie wasn't thrilled to see that word associated with him, he did have to admit that he was getting scared about his health. He also didn't like the way people were beginning to look at him.

Sometimes, standing in front of the mirror after a shower, Eddie said to himself, "I'm just a fat blob. Sometimes I think I am disappearing into all the flab and I'll never find myself again."[2]

Weak Engagements with the Will

Friends and family witnessed or heard Eddie trying numerous coping mechanisms to get the upper hand on food, his increased weight, his diminished energy, and his falling personal confidence:

- I try to go to Weight Watchers meetings.
- I try to put off eating for fifteen minutes, and I usually get over the desire.
- I try not to buy junk food.
- I try not to bring sweets into the house.
- I try not to snack between meals.
- I try to eat a lighter supper in the evening.
- I try to stay away from foods that tempt me.
- I try to remove myself from the kitchen and go for a walk.
- When I'm anxious, I tend to snack. I try to busy myself with little stuff to hold off eating until mealtime. It works occasionally.[3]

I call these decisions and activities *weak engagements with the will*. I label them as such not because they are worthless. They actually can be very useful for the short term. They become *weak* when they are all we do, all we rely on.

What is wrong with them? Look again at the last sentence in the list: *It works occasionally*. These tactics work only intermittently because they are rooted in *trying harder*, without becoming an essentially different person—the kind of person who could and would do right. What we need is a spiritual workout, a set of spiritual *exercises* that fundamentally strengthen our whole inner being, not just our will. It is vital that we make our way in this direction because 55 percent[4] of Americans are overeating like Eddie.

Bodily Desires

Our ancient Christian ancestors considered fasting from food as key to learning how to battle sexual lust. That's one reason why a fasting routine was so common. Asceticism (the principles and practices of self-denial) in one area teaches you asceticism in others: it conditions you to say no to yourself. For the purposes of this chapter, let's make Eating Eddie represent all human bodily desires.

The first thing to say about bodily desires is that they are not automatically wrong, bad, or sinful. In chapter 2, I introduced you to Screwtape and his trainee, Wormwood. One of their conversations reveals the key thought that most disordered desires and most temptations have their roots in something good. The master devil put it like this: "Never forget that when we are dealing with any pleasure in its healthy and normal and satisfying form, we are, in a sense, on [God's] ground."[5]

For instance, to have a desire for food, companionship, or sex is not a sin. To think about something—to have a thought pass through your mind—is not a sin. To find someone physically, emotionally, or spiritually attractive is not a sin. Most temptation does not come from things that are obviously evil. Who among us is tempted to be a serial murderer or a rapist or the director of a global Ponzi scheme? No, we are tempted by things that are good in their proper place: food, shopping, sex, wine, recreation, and entertainment.

Even temptation itself is not wrong. You may be tempted to take something that is not yours; you may be sexually tempted, and so on. None of these experiences is a sin. But to nurture and encourage greedy or sexual desire, to fertilize it so that it leads to craving for more opportunities to cultivate desire—that is sin, whether you took the stuff or practiced some sort of illicit sex or not. As Dallas Willard says, "It is the purposeful entertaining and stimulation of desire that Jesus marks as the manifestation of a sexually improper condition of the soul."[6]

Purposeful entertaining and stimulation are also the basis for, and backdrop to, the biblical command to "not let sin reign in your mortal body so that you obey its evil desires" (Romans 6:12). In plain English this verse points to an important point regarding temptation: your body is a part of this battle because it is the vehicle through which you do life— speak, listen, touch, be touched, and so on. All too often, however, we let sin rule the day in our bodies.

God is always on our side in the moment of temptation. At the intersection of *temptation* and *sin*, God gives us a yellow light to warn us. Some of us think this light means *be cautious, prepare to stop what you are doing*. Others think the yellow light means *floor it, pedal to the metal!* Few people who floor it through an intersection on a yellow light do so acting only on impulse. This decision to floor it is almost never a first decision; it is usually the last decision, a decision rooted in disordered thoughts, feelings, and desires such as, *I am in a hurry, and I must not be thwarted*. It is the strong desire to not be thwarted that becomes sin. The yellow light and endangering others is just the specific context in which we can express the strong and wrong desire in our heart.

Strong Desire

As I mentioned earlier, the New Testament Greek term for lust is *epithumia*. It often means strong, but out-of-line, inordinate desire. To think more about this in the context of bodily desire, let's move away from the bodily desire for food and talk a bit about the bodily desire for sex. Appropriate sexual desire becomes disordered desire (*epithumia*) when, for my own momentary gratification, I turn a woman (or for women, a man) into an object of my indulgence. I want to possess something of her for my enjoyment. This is not at all the same thing as mutually loving sex between married persons. It's self-indulgent, exploitative, and dehumanizing. It is less the obsession to love than to possess, an exercise of domination.[7]

But we must be careful here not to throw *epithumia* out of our lives altogether. As we said about desire in an earlier chapter, Christian spiritual transformation does not call for the flat-out elimination of desire, or even strong desire. *Epithumia* can be used in the positive sense of *eagerness*. For instance, in Luke 22:15 Jesus says to his disciples, "I have eagerly desired to eat this Passover with you before I suffer." In Philippians 1:23 Paul, using the term *epithumia*, says, "I desire to depart and be with Christ." Strong desire to achieve good outcomes in the world is of course valid. Psalm 10:17 says, "The Lord hears the *desire* of the afflicted." Psalm 20:4 asks the Lord to "give you the *desire* of your heart." Psalm 37:4 encourages us to "take delight in the LORD, and he will give you the *desires* of your heart" (emphasis added).

Don't let the knowledge that wrong desires are bad masters

cause you to altogether throw out all desires—even strong ones. The godly task is to turn inordinate desires into strong desires for the good, the better, and even the best things in life.

Turn the concern on its head for a minute. When I use the visual image of a woman to entertain myself, my problem is not that I love her *too much*. The problem is I love her *too little*. My desire for her is disordered because proper strong desire for her would be biblical love: wanting what is good for her and serving her, not using her for my disordered satisfaction. C. S. Lewis has a helpful illustration of this point:

> It would seem that our Lord finds our desires not too strong, but too weak. We are half-hearted creatures, fooling around with drink and sex and ambition when infinite joy is offered us, like an ignorant child who wants to go on making mud pies in a slum because he cannot imagine what is meant by the offer of a holiday at sea.
>
> We are too easily pleased.[8]

Lewis would say that looking to desire is a weak way of being human, with a weak and small payoff: a moment of recreation, not even remembered the next day. The holiday at sea offered to me means becoming the kind of person who so loves others that using them is not an option.

Strong Engagement with the Whole Self

Above I called the list of things overeaters do to try to not eat "weak engagements with the will." I wasn't being mean.

Reliable guidance and helpfulness are what I was shooting for. And I have a sound motive for doing so. The weakness of which I accuse others, I learned the hard way.

As anyone who struggles with lust knows, strong disordered desires become strong shackles and bonds. Looking *in order to* lust is an easy habit to create and extremely difficult to break. As the ancient Christian sage Prudentius put it, "The man [or woman] who casts longing eyes on his neighbor's [wife or daughter, husband or son] is being led in shackles . . . fettered with a thousand chains . . . and yet does not realize that he is [given] over to a cruel bondage."[9]

I was converted at nineteen, right about the time experts say male libido peaks. Great. I was hopeless, "toast" as we say. I had spent the prior six or seven years diligently searching for every sexual escapade a boy of those ages could manage without getting caught by store clerks, my parents, or the girl's parents. Now I was caught in one of the devil's best traps. As Screwtape said, "Tough periods of human [ups and downs] provide excellent opportunity for all sensual temptations, particularly those of sex."[10]

That is true—I can testify to that long and loud. Back in the day I could find eye temptations of all types in all kinds of situations: in the classroom, in the gym, walking between classes, in the dorms or cafeteria, before baseball practice, after practice, at my part-time jobs—even at church. There were babes there too!

But now I was a new, born-again Christian. I genuinely wanted to be different. I sincerely wanted to be a new person, to experience what a "born-again" life was like. The night I was converted, I made huge changes in my sexual ethics and practices that have stayed solidly with me since. But I had this one unbreakable bad habit: if there was a girl in my field of vision, I *had* to check her out. I was fettered and shackled with a thousand chains to a pattern, to a habit that seemed impossible to conquer.

I tried all the usual weak strategies in an effort to use my will to control my eyes. These are true stories:

- I walked with my head down, eyes to the ground, until the day I bruised my inner thigh on one of those big bolts that stick out from yellow fire hydrants.
- I walked around campus with my eyes fixed on nothing in particular on the horizon, until the day I sprained my ankle awkwardly stepping off a curb.
- I reviewed notes from class or read textbooks as I walked, until I scratched myself in the middle of a row of bushes.

These, my fellow strugglers with temptation, are weak attempts at dealing with sin; in my case, the sin of looking to lust to entertain myself. I'll have much more help to offer later in the book, but for now let me give you one example showing why working with the will alone is a weak strategy. My eyes were not the real problem. My eyes were simply obeying my strong *emotional* need for amusement, diversion, and distraction. It is not for nothing that C. S. Lewis has Screwtape telling Wormwood that when Christians get "less dependent on emotion," they are "much harder to tempt."[11]

And that little litany of weak attempts only covers sexual attraction. It leaves untouched my pride, jealousy, arrogance, greed, and dishonesty. I'm telling you, if temptation were a hot jet engine, I was a heat-seeking missile! I didn't need any dark evil to be tempted—all I had to do was get up every day and start moving around in my little world.

Once I learned more about the role of disordered desires, I could see a more doable way to "flee the *evil desires* of youth and pursue righteousness, faith, love and peace, along with those who call on the Lord out of a pure heart" (2 Timothy 2:22, emphasis added). I was on a new path to control the inner compulsions—thoughts, feelings, and memories—that were controlling my eyes.

Media Mary knows something about how thoughts and feelings badger our wills into pursuing inordinate desire. She can also tell us how acting on sinful craving actually shrinks pleasure while enlarging desire.

Ancient and Fruitful Practice

This chapter used eating as the primary metaphor for disordered bodily appetites of all kinds. The prayer below from Saturday Compline leads us to the truth that God will care for us as we journey away from these appetites. It is crucial that you know this in an experiential way. Pray each line with an emphasis on God giving you what you need on your journey.

May God shield me;
may God fill me;
may God keep me;
may God watch me;
may God bring me this night [day]
to the nearness of his love.[12]

SEVEN

MEDIA
MARY

*When we are obedient, God guides
our steps . . . and our stops.*
—CORRIE TEN BOOM[1]

I must confess, in public, to something everyone close to me knows: I am a Facebook minimalist. I have a page and I've got more than four thousand friends, but I rarely post anything and I hardly know how to use the tools on my homepage. I do not get e-mail or text messages to tell me something happened on my page. My wife and daughter set up my profile. I am such a media loser that I just had to yell down the hall to my wife, "Babes, what's that site on the web on which you can watch TV shows?" "Hulu," came back the answer. I think I heard a slight undertone of "the poor dear doesn't know what Hulu is."

But I am curious about all the fuss over Facebook, YouTube, Twitter, and the other outlets for social connectivity. Thus I asked a few friends of mine, whom I know to be big users of social media, to tell me their stories. To keep their identities private, we'll roll their stories into one, and call this person Media Mary.[2]

Three years ago I had never heard of a "status update," and I had not "tagged" anyone since the fifth-grade playground—and I'd never tagged anyone in a picture. Now, after hitting the floor in the morning, the first place my feet stop—well, after the bathroom—is my computer desk. Many mornings I have sat there so long that I had to go without my shower in order to not be late to work. That made for bad hair days, and as hard as that is on my ego, I have to admit that it is a close call as to which I'd hate more: bad hair or not connecting with my Facebook community. I try to check Facebook throughout the day at work, probably about six to eight times per day. I know I've had some close calls with my supervisor almost catching me. But I mostly check at breaks and lunchtime. In between, I check quickly so I don't get caught.

I am getting a little worried, however, but kind of mad too. My family and friends are starting to bug me about how much time I spend on the computer. I admit I do have alerts sent to my phone and my e-mail at work in order to notify me of the activity on my page. I must also admit this is sometimes causing me to lose focus on the people and events of my life. When the activities of life or some person keep me from getting online, I do find myself getting angry, sad, and depressed. Being offline makes me feel disconnected from life. Maybe my family is right: I am getting tired and cranky from losing sleep from being online so late at night.

And that is just the Facebook part of my life. I've now discovered sites where I can search photos of my old friends. On Hulu I can watch the TV shows I missed. YouTube is full of searchable, entertaining, and educational videos. The websites I have discovered over the last few years are great for me! In contrast to today's full offerings of media, when I grew up we had only about a dozen TV channels. Besides that, there were several AM radio stations, and soon thereafter FM radio became a big hit as a source for popular music. Now I never lack for stimulating content and connection in my life. After I check all my sites and watch all my shows, if I find myself wanting more, there are always video games.

I have my days when I think I should listen to the people around me who love me. In the past several months I have tried to:

- *Just shut off the computer and go to bed*
- *Put the computer in the basement to avoid opening it in the morning*
- *Just walk away from the computer to find something else to do*

- *Give myself a talking to and tell myself I don't need this stuff[3]*

What bothers me is that none of this is working. I feel trapped. It is as if ropes come off my computer screen and tie me to my chair. Before I know it, it is three o'clock in the morning. I feel stupid. Why would I risk the ire of my bosses and the career I worked so hard for in graduate school? In addition, I often wonder what it is I want so badly and if the penalties I am paying and losses I am enduring are worth being online all the time?

A couple of weeks ago a thought occurred to me, but I haven't been able to really dig into it: I wonder if, somewhere deep in my subconscious mind, I am making up for a feeling of being cut off from life? I know I spent most of my years in high school and college thinking that everyone else was more connected than I was, having more fun and enjoying life more. I've never wanted to think of myself in those needy ways, but maybe it is leaking out in my behavior.

Proponents and Opponents

Do you know people with Mary's story? It's a safe bet that you do. I was not surprised to read the Barna survey that revealed that 44 percent[4] of Americans say they are tempted to spend too much time on computer-based media.

Mary's family and friends are not alone in their concern

about a loved one's addiction to social media and web-based entertainment. A therapist interviewed for CNN said, "Last Friday, I had three clients in my office with Facebook problems. . . . It's turned into a compulsion—a compulsion to disassociate from your real world and go live in the Facebook world." The therapist continued, "Problems arise when users ignore family and work obligations because they find the Facebook world a more enjoyable place to spend time than the real world."[5]

When I consider the conversations I am hearing in academic circles, I see a divide emerging among both students and scholars. Some thoughtful people say Twitter, Facebook, and other forms of social media don't connect people, that they actually isolate them from reality. Other equally intelligent people say social media does indeed connect people, and that cynics and doubters are wrong, that such people are just slow to pick up on the new realities of communication. The article in CNN, taking the side of the defenders, said, "Emails, Twitter, and Facebook have led to more communication, not less—especially for people who may have trouble meeting in the real world because of great distance or social difference."[6]

I have tried to remain open-minded about this debate. In theory I see both sides. But more concretely I have to admit that I see a growing trend of relational dysfunction in online conversations. I read people's posts on various media and see them saying the most horrible things I have ever heard. I am a hundred percent sure that most of the online diatribes would never be said to someone's face. Beyond this I am hearing about cases of full-on addiction to web-based entertainment and connectivity. It seems ironic and counterintuitive that in a sphere where *connection* is the stated goal, imprisonment and *self-absorption* are a common outcome.

I see something in play here, a typical device of evil. When it comes to online connectivity, we may have fallen into the classic trap of the devil. Screwtape, advising Wormwood on how to wreck a man's soul, says, "An ever increasing craving for an ever diminishing pleasure is the formula."[7] When Lewis wrote those words, he had in mind the search for and the novelty of constant change in contemporary church services. I think the same thing applies to our search for the latest video game, smartphone, or other device.

Screwtape goes on to explain to Wormwood, "The demand for constant change diminishes pleasure while increasing desire. The pleasure of novelty costs money, so that the desire for it spells [greed] or unhappiness or both. And . . . the more rapacious this desire, the sooner it must eat up all the innocent sources of pleasure and pass on to those [God] forbids."[8]

This is a train you don't want to board. Get off quick if you've already found your seat.

You Don't Have to Do It

Mary is not a *victim* of evil inventions. She is not trapped because a machine and the software being run on it are wicked. Both those things are amoral. They are creating neither virtue nor vice until we do something with them. With them we reach out to a loved one or reach for our favorite form of sexual titillation. With the exception of a few addictions that are based in biological or chemical malfunctions, none of us are victims of sin. We are creators of sin. Sin is created when our wrong desires match up with the tempting possibilities of our lives.

It is important that you understand and believe what I just wrote. You must reject the notion that you are a hopeless victim and powerless in the face of temptation. You don't *have* to do it. If you are struggling to believe this, hang with me for a few more sentences—you'll get it.

Think of the last time you were tempted to gossip: Would you do it if someone had a knife to your throat? Would you repeat the morsel of gossip upon pain of death? No, of course not. Why? Because a different, more powerful *want* (to not have your throat slit) overtook your previous *want* (to gossip). The knife and threat changed that faculty in you that arranges and orders desire, what Dallas Willard calls your *wanter*. If you were about to lie at work to cover up a mistake, to blame it on an innocent colleague, would you tell the lie if a deadly, poisonous snake, held to your face, would strike your cheekbone at the first whisper of a lying syllable? When something more powerful than what you thought you wanted comes into view, it causes you to repent and to rethink your actions.

Knowing that your wanter is controlling you and that your wanter can be changed are crucial first steps to victory over temptation. This is so because the core thought behind most temptation is this: *If I don't do this or that thing, I am going to miss out on something wonderful, great, necessary, and fulfilling to my real self.* Not missing out on a possibility that sounded wonderful was a large motivation in the fall of Eve, as she was tempted to be more than what God had created her to be. But this fear is *the Big Lie*. On the contrary, the available, livable truth is this: *God takes care of me! He is my shepherd. I shall not be in want! No matter the context, situation, case, or circumstance before me, if I have made the Lord my shepherd, I am everywhere and always safe with what I have.*

Can you see now how this works? Why do 60 percent of Americans battle anxiety, fear, and worry? Because they are not safe. They do not have the Lord as their shepherd, not really. They have him only in an occasional reading of a psalm that celebrates the Lord's shepherding of King David of the Old Testament. But we can get there. We can renovate our wanters and reorder our desires. A quote from Willard has stuck with me for a number of years, giving me an image for what such a life would look like:

> The person who happily lets God be God . . . knows and deeply accepts the fact that their feelings, of whatever kind, do not have to be fulfilled. They spend little time grieving over non-fulfillment . . . they get off the conveyor belt of emotion and desire when it first starts to move toward the buzz saw of sin.[9]

Stop It—Turn It Off!

Thoughts and feelings on one foot and desire on the other work together like pedals on a bike. One (thoughts and feelings) makes the other (desire) go. The reverse is also true.

Sometimes desire works on our brains and emotions. This round-and-round activity can make lots of emotional and mental noise. I have a vivid picture of this from my boyhood. Anyone born in the fifties and riding a bicycle in the sixties knows that playing cards clipped to the sides of a bicycle frame, poking into the spokes, create a flapping noise that, to a child's imaginative ears, is similar to the sound of a motor-cycle engine.

If you've got incessant noise like that going on in your head and heart, stop it—turn it off! Stop to think about how ridiculous and harmful sinful desires are. Put the snake near your face. Actually it's already there; you just can't see it. Work on your wanter.

Your present desires don't have to rule. They don't *have* to mean anything. Get some new desires. Use your thoughts and feelings as allies. They don't always have to be enemies. Changing your *thoughts* about something—for instance, decid-ing that helping your daughter with her homework is more important than another round of a video game—will almost always change your *feelings* as well. I also change my thoughts and feelings through reading Scripture, meditation, prayer, and the kinds of exercises I suggest at the end of each chapter. When thoughts and feelings change, your desires will follow right along. You will be free from the tyranny of what you wanted.

Let's take a look at how Lazy Larry, through understand-ing the concepts of Christian spiritual transformation, took some steps down that path.

Ancient and Fruitful Practice

I love and make great use of this Canticle from Midday Prayer in *Celtic Daily Prayer*. Write it out slowly on a sheet of paper, noticing what power each line gives us to rightly order our desires.

Teach us dear Lord, to number our days;
that we may apply our hearts unto wisdom
Oh, satisfy us early with your mercy . . .
Let the beauty of the Lord our God be upon us;
and establish the work of our hands . . . [10]

EIGHT

LAZY
LARRY

*If you think of this world as a place intended
simply for our happiness, you find it quite
intolerable: think of it as a place of training and
correction and it's not so bad.*

—C. S. LEWIS[1]

I'm not braggin', just sayin': I don't have to be concerned
about being lazy. I have to be alert to a lack of rest and
remember to rest on the Sabbath; I need to remember to be
satisfied by doing a modest day's work and to be happy with
its outcomes, trusting God for the work that remains. Since
you are reading a book on temptation, you are probably a
motivated person yourself. But you and I both can still learn
from Lazy Larry.

By now you may be able to guess why this is true. Larry's
real problem is not his outward laziness. It is the inward desire
from which the idleness comes. Larry is a composite of adult

students I have taught over the last five years. Their profiles and personalities have stuck with me.

> *Larry says that it has always been a mystery to him how people can spend hours in the library studying when great parties are going on down the block in the dorm rooms or apartments. How do doctors keep seeing patients when the sun is out and lying in the sand is good?*
>
> *"I honestly do not get it," he told me. Continuing on, he said, "the sun, the sand, and a towel pull on me more than a magnet pulls on iron shavings."*
>
> *"Just the thought of exertion exhausts me," he admitted. "I cannot picture myself doing it. When I try to see myself being active, I feel frustrated and angry. I don't want to have to dance to the music of this world. I want to relax, chill, and avoid all the activity I can. No matter how much my mom and dad lecture me, I can't make myself work. I just don't want to. I don't want to deal with this . . . it is just too hard . . . it never works . . . it is just the way I am . . ."*
>
> *After our conversation, Larry wrote me this note: "I don't feel as if I am, as people often say, indifferent. I am just positive in the direction of sleeping as much as I can, lying around when at all possible, watching my favorite television shows, and perhaps looking through a couple of catalogues."*
>
> *When I asked Larry what he did to avoid the temptation to laziness, he said, "Occasionally, when*

someone would really get on my case to get me moving,
I'd try to be and act different. I've tried:

- *Praying about it and reading my Bible*
- *Staying focused and having willpower*
- *Talking myself into getting up and getting going*
- *Pepping myself up*
- *Reminding myself of what I would lose if I didn't*
  get my work done[2]

"As I've pondered why these tactics have let me
down, failing to create lasting change, I've discovered
something surprising. Always thinking of myself as 'my
own man,' it never occurred to me that all the time I
have been trying to be the opposite of my grandfather
who raised me. I watched him work his life away. He
seemed to never have any fun, leisure, or relaxation.
He seemed incapable of it. As a young boy I remem-
ber vowing to never be like him. It seemed like he was
wasting his life on stuff that did not matter—that
fence would need to be repaired again next year; the
barn would need to be cleaned again tomorrow. It's
weird that now I seem to be wasting my life in the other
extreme, at least that is what people tell me."

You, as a motivated reader, and I, as a motivated author,
may not be able to relate to Larry as much as we related to
the snapshots of people in earlier chapters, but 41 percent of
Americans could feel the last few paragraphs in their bones.

A large percentage of the people in your neighborhood fail to use their God-given energy, strength, talents, and gifts. This is very common. Any teacher will tell you that many more students fail due to laziness than due to a lack of ability.

A Truly Deadly Sin

You may not be aware of the fact, but sloth (laziness) is a big deal. Known also as apathy, it is like a capital crime in the spiritual world. It is one of the seven deadly sins—along with lust, gluttony, greed, wrath, envy, and pride. There are several practical reasons laziness sits near the top of the list of all possible sins.

First, someone who is lazy hurts himself or herself most of all. Lazy people miss one of life's best, God-given, abounding experiences—the satisfaction of making a contribution to their job, their family, or a needy person of any kind. Ancient wisdom tells us, "Despite their desires, the lazy will come to ruin, for their hands refuse to work" (Proverbs 21:25 NLT). The ruin in view here includes the death of our spirit, our confidence, and our self-respect. This is so because we were created to work, to be God's collaborative friends. In terms of theological history, divine-human cooperative work came before, and thus supersedes, sin and the fall. To work a hard, but humble and modest, day does not come from sin—it is obedience, and it is faithful to the design of God.

But there is a tricky bit here: our ancient forefathers knew it is possible to be busy and yet slothful.[3] Here is how it works. The ancient Christians had God and his will as their primary point of reference for life, but it's possible to be busy with non-God stuff and be slothful with reference to your spiritual self and the work of God on the earth. While I am sure the vast majority of the respondents to the Barna survey did not have this meaning of sloth in view, we should keep it in view. It may be *the way* many overly busy Americans are slothful.

First, laziness, of both kinds we are considering here, kills us moment by moment, a day at a time. In a destructive and vicious cycle, laziness comes from having no clear purpose to live and causes a person to lose meaningful ways by which to organize a life based on values, priorities, and practices. As one aphorism has it, "A lazy person is already a lifeless person but one who can't be legally buried."[4]

Second, lazy people hurt others. They make life hard for anyone with whom they have contact. The declaration of Scripture is: "People who don't take care of their relatives, and especially their own families, have given up their faith. They are worse than someone who doesn't have faith in the Lord" (1 Timothy 5:8 CEV). This is obviously a very strong statement, the kind of pronouncement not seen all that often in the New Testament.

Third and last, lazy people fail in the most basic of all Christian ways: the failure to love. *Love* is, in the words of Dallas Willard, "the genuine inner readiness and longing to secure the good of others."[5] This love comes only from the inner being of a person transformed into the image of Jesus.

This transformation happens as the gift of God, through the grace of God, and by the common instruments of his grace: word, sacrament, prayer, worship, rightly motivated and correctly practiced spiritual disciplines, community, and so on. Willard writes, "Spiritual formation for the Christian refers to the Spirit-driven process of forming the inner world of the human self in such a way that it becomes like the inner being of Christ himself . . . [and] this is not a human attainment. It is, finally, a gift of grace."[6]

Lazy to the Bone

We live from the unseen depths of our being. We behave from our hearts, our imaginations, our deep dreams, and our fears. What comes out of us in terms of attitudes, words, and deeds, or laziness, as we are considering here, comes from what is often called, in common conversation, the spiritual portion of us. But too often we try to deal with temptation by controlling our environment and our body parts. These tactics are not without merit—in a crisis. But no one lives in crisis mode all the time. You and I need a strategy for dealing with temptation that is doable within our everyday ordinary life.

The fundamental insight we need for such a life comes from Jesus: it is our unseen, inward portions that control our bodies and the body's activities within our surrounding environment. Jesus said: "The good man from his inner good treasure flings forth good things, and the evil man out of his inner evil storehouse flings forth evil things" (Matthew 12:35 AMPLIFIED BIBLE). If we persist in acting contrary to Jesus' wisdom, if we insist on working from the outside in, seeking to control our eyes or our hands without transforming the thoughts, the feelings, and the will that control them, we will predictably fail.

Why? Each of us, at the core of our beings—me as I write, you as you read—is a certain kind or type of person. To deal well with temptation, we must engage in a process of changing that core person, that one part of us that drives the rest of us.

This inward-outward reality is fascinating to me. I, fully trusting the brilliance and competency of Jesus, believe he knew what he was talking about when he said we act—use our bodies—based on whatever reality is *inside* us. But this is the interesting part of spiritual transformation into Christlikeness: most of the spiritual disciplines that transform our inner beings are bodily. Our bodies work with us as allies to transform our hearts, minds, wills, emotions, and social selves. Surprised to hear this? Think about it: fasting is bodily; so is praying, reading, kneeling, seeking solitude, and even keeping silent. As much as I can as I go through my day, I use routine bodily movements (walking, riding my bike, holding the phone, and so on) to connect to something I am working on spiritually.

Changed to the Bone

You know the expression "bad to the bone"? The good news of Jesus is that we can be transformed to the bone and witness profound and lasting change in our hearts, wills, thoughts, and feelings. This is precisely what is in view when I talk about spiritual formation as the basic strategy and tactic for dealing with temptation. In spiritual formation, Dallas Willard says our task is "developing a nature or character that resolutely *chooses* the good." He continues:

> Good persons must live in a world where doing evil is a
> genuine choice for them . . . [But] by ceasing to do evil
> I can make a significant impact on the moral evil that is
> in my world. By trusting the goodness and greatness of
> God, I can turn loose of the chain that drags me into
> moral evil: the chain of self-deification, which puts me in
> the position of the one I trust to take care of me. Nearly
> all evil-doing is done under the guise of "necessity." "I
> wouldn't lie, cheat, steal, hurt others but for the fact that
> it is necessary to secure my aims—which of course *I* must
> bring about."[7]

It is common, when a conversation about spiritual formation starts, for a number of people to say, "I can't do this. I
am too busy. I am already buried under the guilt of not getting the things done I already need to do." I get it—I really
do. But what if the reverse is true? What if pursuing the transformation of our inner character is the best way to reorganize
life, to live well, to accomplish life's tasks and responsibilities
with peace? Have you ever paused to ask yourself: What is
the cost of not dealing with temptation? What is the ongoing
cost of living poorly with disordered desires, inclinations, and
tendencies toward sin?

Every spiritual mentor in the history of Christianity,
from Jesus to Paul to modern sages, has known that working on interior, ultimate issues is what matters most. This
is why Lewis has Screwtape tell Wormwood to strive to get
followers of Jesus to stop being attentive to universal (we
might say *ultimate* issues) in favor of *the stream of immediate*

sense experiences that come routinely to our conscious minds. Screwtape says to Wormwood: "Your business is to fix [the Christian's] attention on the stream [*of immediate sense experiences*]. Teach him to call it 'real life' and don't let him ask what he means by 'real.'"[8] Lewis knows we are susceptible to this tactic because he knows that Christians are apt to "find it all but impossible to believe in the unfamiliar while the familiar is before their eyes."[9]

Finding Freedom in Finding God

The goal of *Our Favorite Sins* is to cause you to want a real experience of the real God so much that your other disordered desires and wants are put in second place. The goal here is not simply to stay away from sin, though that would be a good temporary fix, like wrapping black tape around the steaming leak of a car hose until you can get to a service station. Rather, I have a permanent repair in mind: to steer clear of temptation by reordering your thoughts, feelings, desires, and will by wanting God and wanting to derive your life from and live it within the story he's telling. The wider intention is to become passionately focused on God and his *stuff*. For from God comes a whole new way of living and giving. It is called "living water."

Picture Jesus standing by the drinking fountain in the hallway at work or at school. As a colleague approaches to drink, Jesus says, "Everyone who drinks this water will be thirsty again, but whoever drinks the water I give them will never thirst. Indeed, the water I give them will become in them a

113

spring of water welling up to eternal life . . . whoever believes in me will never be thirsty" (John 4:13–14; 6:35). Jesus then reiterates, "Let anyone who is thirsty come to me and drink" (John 7:37). Substitute the word *desire* for thirst, and crucial ideas for defeating temptation become clear:

- Everyone who desires the water of the world will always desire more and never be satisfied.
- He who receives what Jesus gives—his life as a ransom for yours—will not routinely desire in an unhealthy, disordered way; rather, this person will be filled to the point of brimming over to the good of others.
- Whoever believes Jesus, who trusts in him and places faith and confidence in him and is thirsty for him, is invited to come and drink from the water of his life.

Leave your disordered desires at the bottom of the well of life. Let the worms eat them. Let's us, you and me, go to Jesus and ask for his living water. It is healing for the soul. It transforms desire. It sets the captive free.

Disordered desires imprison us. In the end they give us nothing—not one lasting shred of goodness, freedom, joy, or love. But God, through Jesus, wants us to be utterly free. Why does God care about our freedom? Is he a French philosopher spelling out for the Western world the political doctrine of *liberty*? Hardly! Modern notions of liberty utterly pale in contrast to the liberty God gives. God has something more in mind than political freedom—as wonderful and cherished as that is. God has in mind freedom from destructive desire and deliverance into his kingdom of light and love, loving God with your whole heart, soul, mind, strength, and body—and your neighbor as yourself. Only the truly free go there.

Let's look next then at how we can be freed from the tyranny of our desires, the tyranny of what we want.

Ancient and Fruitful Practice

Every Monday night at bedtime I am delighted to see these two prayers during compline. The first I use to think about my heart, both on that particular day and in general. The second I use to pray against evil: both what I can see within my desires and any stimuli coming at me from without. Try this approach. If it works for you, stick with it for a few days.

Living God of the universe—may the Light of Lights come to my dark heart from Thy place; may the Spirit's wisdom come to my heart's tablet from my Savior.[10]

Circle me, Lord, keep protection near and danger afar . . . Circle me, Lord, keep peace within; keep evil out.[11]

NINE

MODERN AND FUTILE

Our Society is a dangerous network of
domination and manipulation in which we
can easily get entangled and lose our soul.
—HENRI NOUWEN[1]

In this chapter we will examine seven modern and futile
ways of thinking about and dealing with temptation.
Sometimes we are conscious of employing these ineffective
devices. Other times we act from them, but in a subconscious
way. Whatever is the case for you, by being made aware of
them and using the insights you gained in earlier chapters,
you can avoid the seven mistakes below.

1. Underestimating the Power of Desire

Maybe you remember the antidrug commercial from the

eighties. The ad showed a man who held up an egg and said, "This is your brain." He then picked up a frying pan and said, "This is drugs." He then cracked open the egg, fried it in the pan, and said, "This is your brain on drugs." At the end he looked up at the camera and asked, "Any questions?"

Something like this needs to be done for the present recreational use of desire. The most alarming part of our present futility with temptation is that we actually *cultivate* disordered desire. We find it fun. It makes us feel alive. Let me show you how your brain on the drug *desire* works.

I grew up with older siblings. They were between five and nine years older than I. That meant, among other things, that I got introduced at a young age to cool music. As much I love the Beach Boys—they are my all-time favorites—sadly, I have to say they inadvertently taught millions of young people, myself included, to cultivate the wrong forms of desire. The legendary 1966 *Pet Sounds* album features the memorable song "Wouldn't It Be Nice," about star-crossed young lovers who dream of getting married. That's good, right? That's wholesome. Not so fast. It's subtle, but listen: after lamenting that "the more we talk about it, it only makes it worse to live without it," the next line says, "But let's talk about it" before going back to the thematic line, "Wouldn't it be nice?" *We know we can't go there, but let's talk about it anyway.* How can that be good? The song encourages us to cultivate the desire for never-ending kisses, for spending the night together, for doing *everything* we want to do.

I'm sure you can name your own tunes that rooted deep in your spirit, launching you on a lifelong journey of cultivating prohibited desire. Remember "Lay, Lady, Lay" from Bob Dylan? After suggesting the woman get comfortable on his bed, he sings:

> *Why wait any longer for the world to begin?*
> *You can have your cake and eat it too.*

I'm not bashing Brian Wilson, Bob Dylan, or—if you're younger than me—today's entertainers. My iPod is full of their tunes. But I am saying that encouragements to disordered desires are all around us, all the time. And the intentional cultivation of desire is the place where Americans are the most futile in our dealings with temptation. Too many of us think: *Desire doesn't really matter; after all, it is only a thought, aspiration, feeling, or wish of the heart. Surely,* we miscalculate, *it is actions, deeds, and behaviors that count. Not something merely interior such as desire.* On the contrary, the Bible offers this wisdom on desire: "The righteousness of the upright delivers them, but the unfaithful are trapped by evil desires" (Proverbs 11:6).

The problem is that if you cultivate the wrong desires, when temptation presents (and it presents often), it makes it all the more likely you'll fall headlong into sin. You can't flirt with this stuff. Wrong desires are just waiting for the right opportunities.

There are three issues of the Christian life: orthodoxy, orthopraxy, and orthopathos.[2] Most of us know that orthodoxy is right thinking or right theology. Orthopraxy is fairly well understood too; it refers to right practices. But *orthopathos*, what does that mean? It is rightly ordered passions, feelings, and desires. It is precisely what we are shooting for in this book. This analogy might help you get an image of what I have in mind: just as orthopedic doctors straighten broken parts of our skeleton, so we can walk well, so do straight, aligned-to-Jesus desires help us live well.[3]

Rightly ordered passions and desires are the only long-term strategy for dealing with temptation. Every other approach will provide short-term help at best or will let you down completely. Avoiding temptation seems so hard when the system of desire within us is powerfully aligned with sin and thus bent to act on temptation. But you do not need to stay in that position. Millions of followers of Jesus over the past two thousand years have found that when they follow Jesus, their system of desires is rewired and they receive freedom from the allure of various temptations.

2. "I'm Different, so It Won't Happen to Me"

I don't believe in slippery slopes. Too often, thinking in terms of slippery slopes puts the responsibility for the downward slide on the slope itself. I prefer to think in terms of *steps*, like the steps down to your basement or the steps down from your front porch to the walkway leading to the sidewalk. The image of steps leaves us feeling in charge of the journey. The image of slopes makes us feel out of control.

To defeat temptation, you must discover, realize, acknowledge, and confess that (1) aside from the rare chemical addiction, you *have been* in control of your life and (2) you *are* in control right now. Without this knowledge, obtained through experience (not just "head knowledge," as we say), you are not likely to fight your inner demons. It is essential that you know that you can turn around and march right back up the steps you've been walking down. It takes a bit more effort to go up, but the solid footing of the porch and the view of life it provides are well worth it.

For people in positions of responsibility, such as parents, managers, teachers, and others, the setup for following temptation into sin—whether deceit, worry, substance abuse, or sexual immorality—often follows a pattern. Let me show you, based on my long observations and self-knowledge, how I think the descending steps unfold:

1. Being created in the image of God, we have a strong, innate, and instinctive desire to use our God-given gifts, creativity, and human energy. We desire the capacity to be a force for good in the world. We want to actually have the freedom and ability to do this within our chosen endeavors. So far, so good.

2. In working toward this upright goal, things change under the duress caused by too many challenges or too much success. We find ourselves doing too much work, taking on too much responsibility, and giving out too much empathy. In short, we hit the intellectual and, more commonly, the emotional and spiritual limitations all of us have.

3. Next comes a desire for diversion from this pain, for *entertainment*, for something that will take

our attention off the ache and confusion. We want pleasure, not heartache.

4. The desire for diversion, to be distracted from pain and burnout, leads us into temptation.

5. The trap being thus set, sin crouching at our door, we are caught. We are trapped in the self-destructive behaviors and addictions that latched onto our desire to medicate pain. These "medications" end up destroying careers, partnerships, friendships, marriages, and families.

Disgraced politicians, corrupt business leaders, and fallen pastors are all the evidence we need of the personal and collateral damage caused when this five-step pattern goes unchecked. But how do we stop this pattern? By breaking the cycle before step 3. We cannot let our desire to succeed, achieve, or win override our desire to be the right kind of person. To do the common thing, to rationalize winning at all costs, is to make the most shortsighted, life-damning decision a person can make. If a wrong choice is made at step 3, all manner of destructive chaos is unleashed. The surrounding damage is often stunning to behold.

3. Believing That Keeping It Real Is Most Valuable

I'm not sure why the attitude I've identified a couple of times in this book as "just keep it real" has gained such a foothold in our society, but it has. Maybe it is a child of moral relativism. Perhaps it comes from the exhaustion and accompanying cynicism of trying to deal with temptation in wrong and futile ways.

Of course, the idea is not all bad. As a statement against falsity it is admirable. But when the "real" being protected is not *good*, we are wading into a dangerous current of water. But for the sake of discussion here, let's agree for the moment with the idea that fighting temptation is a losing cause and that "just keeping it real" is better. Do we then just tell someone to get over it when his or her spouse couldn't escape the temptation of having an affair with Mr. or Ms. Right? After all, as some argue, the offending spouse, being defenseless, couldn't help himself or herself and shouldn't even try, given that keeping it real is supposedly the highest ethical concern. If avoiding temptation is an unachievable goal, what is one to do when faced with Mr. or Ms. Right?

Let's make this personal. Let's say for the sake of discussion that you are the one arguing for keeping it real. All right, let's now say you own a family business that has the potential to make a nice little profit. Let's say the business is a local frozen yogurt shop and that you work on very small margins. And because you are just starting, and burning quickly through your first round of capital, your business model has zero ability to swallow any losses from employee theft.

But Sally just can't keep her hands out of the cash register. She takes only twenty or thirty dollars a day, but that adds up to seven or eight thousand dollars a year. Worse yet, she has convinced her fellow employees Keith, Tony, and Allison that because you are a franchised corporation, you don't need the money and won't miss it. Just keepin' it real.

So now you've got thirty thousand dollars a year going out the door. That is money you could use to put your kids through college, save for retirement, or take your family on vacation. But don't be too hard on your young employees—they simply could not imagine resisting the temptation of the *corporate* cash in the *corporate* drawer.

It quickly becomes obvious that no one advocating keeping it real means it in actuality. It sounds good on first hearing. No more tough choices. No more personal discipline. No more self-reflections on the less-than-ideal aspects of our inner persons. It also sounds good if we are the *actor*. But once we become *the acted upon*, we quickly develop an alternative worldview.

4. Failing to Admit We Are Prone to Wander

A favorite hymn contains the lyric, "Prone to wander—Lord, I feel it—prone to leave the God I love."[4] To be *prone* to something means to have the tendency toward it; to be naturally inclined toward a given thing; to be disposed to engage in a given activity; or to have an inclination of heart, mind, or will in the direction of a substance or interest. If I review my life, I am reminded that I have been prone to a few unhelpful, sometimes unholy things.

At about twelve I discovered that an uncle we visited on occasion had *Playboy* magazines in the wooden periodical holder that sat beside his recliner. Granted, *Playboy* in 1968 was really tame compared to the pornography of today, but even a girl in a sexy swimsuit or nightgown could get my juvenile heart pumping and hormones racing.

This gateway experience primed me for further bad behavior at the job I got at a local drug store when I was sixteen. I delivered prescriptions to shut-ins and helped restock the shelves. I liked the restocking part a lot, especially when the book and magazine vendors would leave old copies of smutty magazines and books up in the attic. On breaks or after work I could fill my mind and heart with lots of less-than-ideal thoughts. Prone to wander—yes, I feel it! I knew it was wrong the whole time. But my desire for the sexual stimulation easily, no contest, overrode any desire I might have had to be good.

But there is more than just the typical sexual stuff. I am bent toward repetitive, addictive athletic behavior too. For instance, I was instantly hooked the first time I hit a round ball with a round bat—squarely. The feeling is amazing. The ball seemed to jump off the bat. Same thing with golf—I swear I think I felt something primordial leap within me the first time I compressed a golf ball correctly, felt the sensation in my hands and arms, heard the distinct sound, and saw the beautiful sight of proper ball flight. My favorite pastime as a young teenager was shooting baskets in my driveway. The sound of the ball swishing through the net as I practiced free throws reverberated in me like the kick drum or bass guitar does at a loud concert. These activities called out to the addictive desires of my heart.

Prone to wander, yes, indeed I feel it. You probably do

too. You could insert your stories in place of mine. But now I want you to know something I have experienced in the forty years since I was a teenager: prone to follow Jesus is possible too. The hymn I quoted at the beginning of this section tells how to begin: "Here's my heart Lord, take and seal it, seal it for thy courts above."

Getting up from the deadweight of the prone position takes some effort. But look up: see the outstretched, nail-scarred hands of Jesus reaching out to pull you up. Jesus and those cosmically strong hands are God's gracious power, there to lift your burdened soul off the dirty deck of life.

5. Trying to Drink from a Dried-Up Well[5]

Jesus said, "Anyone who drinks the water I give will never thirst—not ever. The water I give will be an artesian spring within, gushing fountains of endless life" (John 4:14 MSG).

These words of Jesus, this great visionary promise of his, alert us to a crucial, determinative fact regarding temptation. Dealing with temptation begins with a straightforward but weighty choice: what is ultimate? If your answer is "my desires," that leads to a certain kind of life. That kind of life is like a thirsty man drifting on the ocean in a life raft. Drinking salt water not only makes him thirst again, but it also kills him. This is a powerful picture of the destruction of disordered desires. Drinking salt water *seems* to be the right and reasonable thing to do. "After all, I am *so* thirsty, and what else around me has the capacity to quench my thirst?" asks the man or woman who cannot see past his or her disordered desires. "All I can see around me for miles toward every horizon is water. What else I am to do?"

But think with me: drinking *that* water is such a sad and brutal delusion. Those waters make demands that our bodies cannot bear. Those waters, those out-of-order desires, are cruel to the point of spiritual death. Malformed structures of desire within the human person are like ancient deities that one might see in a movie. They tantalize. They get us in their grip with the promise of satisfying an urge that seems important to us at the time. But as the drama unfolds, we find these gods are mean and unreliable. Far from satisfying us, they consume us upon *their* desires.

Consider Jesus' words again: "Everyone who drinks this water will get thirsty again and again. Anyone who drinks the water I give will never thirst—not ever. The water I give will be an artesian spring within, gushing fountains of endless life" (John 4:13–14 MSG).

Do you think Jesus was imparting knowledge—or just spouting cool-sounding, religious maxims? Do you think he knew what he was talking about? If your honest-to-the-bones answer is "yes, I believe he did know, and does know what he is talking about, and I do think he is giving us real knowledge on which to base a spiritual life of following him"—well then, you are on the right track. If, however, these words of Jesus are not understandable to you, or if you cannot bring yourself to act as if they are true, right, and good—well then, to one degree or another you are leaving yourself vulnerable to your desires, those fickle, cruel gods that reside in each of us and rule us with unmitigated thirst. Until we change the source of our water.

6. Forgetting That Temptations Oversell and Underdeliver

We are futile in the face of temptation because we believe it. But temptations are worse liars than Tommy Flanagan, the Jon Lovitz character in the funny skits from the late 1980s on *Saturday Night Live*. Tommy is a pathological liar who says things like:

> I didn't always lie. No, when I was a kid, I told the truth. But then one day, I got caught stealing money out of my mother's purse. I lied. I told her it was homework—that my teacher told me to do it. And she got fired! Yeah, that's what happened! After that, lying was easy for me. I lied about my age and joined the army. I was thirteen at the time. Yeah . . . I went to Vietnam, and I was injured catching a mortar shell in my teeth. And they made me a three-star general! . . . Yeah, that's the ticket . . . Yeah, you betcha![6]

Perhaps the chief power of temptations is their ability to lie to us. Temptations always oversell and underdeliver. Let's get real, maybe even a little raw, about this to make the point abundantly clear. A lonely traveling salesman, several states away from home, feeling sexually deprived by his wife, decides to use the services of a prostitute or to have a drunken hookup with his female coworker. When considering just the act of sex, of whatever sort one would choose, the average liaison of this sort lasts somewhere between ten and thirty minutes. Tell me: is it worth it? No matter how great the sex may be, is it worth losing the following things?

- Your marriage
- The respect of your parents
- The admiration of your siblings
- The high opinion of your children
- The respect of your colleagues
- Your job (by violating company policy)
- Your basic reputation in your community
- The ability of others to trust you
- Your self-esteem
- Your health (by possibly contracting sexually transmitted diseases)
- The health of your spouse (by possibly passing on STDs)

Temptation will never level with you or be straight with you. It is a one-note instrument. Temptation only says this: "I can help you, right now, to fulfill that deep and strong desire in you." Temptation is a tool in the arsenal of Satan. And the first friends of Jesus, who saw the work of Satan firsthand, tell us, "Be alert and of sober mind. Your enemy the devil prowls around like a roaring lion looking for someone to devour" (1 Peter 5:8). Don't expect temptation to tell you, "I'm lying in wait over here . . ." As Max Lucado has written, "Satan numbs our awareness and short-circuits our self-control . . . in a fog of weakness."[7]

Don't ever count on temptation to be fair. It will never fully disclose the outcomes of yielding to it. Temptation doesn't care about you. Your future is of no concern to it. Temptation lives for the moment. Victory over temptation requires that, at a minimum, we have a larger view in mind than just the moment at hand. Because temptation is so dangerous to our souls, Jesus taught us to pray, "Lead us not into temptation," or as *The Message* has it, "Keep us safe from ourselves and the Devil" (Matthew 6:13).

This prayer, as Dallas Willard says, "expresses the understanding that we cannot stand up under much pressure . . . it is a vote of no confidence in our own abilities . . . so we are asking for pity . . . in the form of protection from circumstances."[8] Dietrich Bonhoeffer understands the prayer to mean something like this: don't let me get to that place in which I am completely abandoned by whatever spiritual strength I have and then left alone by God as well "with the loss of all strength, defenseless, delivered into Satan's hands."[9]

The scholarly treatments of this last part of the Lord's Prayer are varied and beyond the scope of this book, but my best understanding of the passage is this: *Never let me get to the place where I am given over to my desires, where I would let my desires give birth to sin and sin to death.* This is in line with the historic prayers of God's people before and during the time of Jesus. Sincere Jews, who loved God and sought obedience to him, prayed these prayers every morning and evening:

Bring me not into the power of sin . . .
And not into the power of guilt
And not into the power of temptation
And not into the power of anything shameful.[10]

Don't get duped by temptation. Step out of the futility. Take it as seriously as a snake. And recognize that God's intention is never that we fall into sin. He will always provide a way out of our temptation and deliver us from evil. Take *that* way.

7. Not Understanding That Daily Devotions Can Be Futile Too

The heading above may have made you say, "huh?" You may have been tempted to write me off as a heretic. But give me a chance. Let me show you what I mean, and I think you'll easily agree with me. This is our one last bit of work to do with the issue of futility.

The big idea is that daily devotions, sometimes called morning devotions, *alone* will rarely deliver us from temptation. They *could*, but they seldom *do*. Here's why: we don't even *intend* daily devotions to do such a thing! Second, morning devotions are often completely disconnected from the rest of our lives. And regarding temptation, it is our actual life that is in view, not just morning prayers. For too many people I have known, sincere Christians trying to do the right thing, daily devotions often make only the margins—the early mornings or the late nights—of our lives spiritual. They too often leave the middle of our lives, the main parts, untouched.

But having said all that, I would never advise someone to stop doing morning or evening prayer. In fact the remainder of this book advises the complete opposite. And I practice them both nearly every day. What I advise is that we rethink *the role* of daily devotions.

I suggest rethinking daily devotions in this way: Don't reduce your spiritual life to them. Don't let your quiet times be the sum total of your spiritual life. Rather, consider morning and evening prayer to be like pillars upon which you build daily, transformative practices. I'll tell you what I do.

In the morning I engage in some form of prayer or spiritual exercises. Almost every night I say compline prayers from *Celtic Daily Prayer*.[11] But these two brief spiritual practices do not *constitute* my life with God, my followership of Jesus, or my walk in the Spirit. *They enable them.* They are like great, large pillars that allow me to build a life that consists of an ongoing, everyday, conversational relationship with God. Morning and evening prayer are the irreducible minimums that facilitate alertness, discernment, and prayer throughout my busy days as I go, with God, from one complex leadership task to another.

Here is one last idea for how I make daily devotions fruitful not futile: Instead of using them to avoid temptation and to stop sinning, I use them to remind me of my role in the story of God, to get me active in doing good deeds of love and service. I use them to remind me that my actual life counts too, not just the prayer that happens on the morning or evening margins. In this way I do not have to add a bunch of busyness to do good in the world. My world, my actual present life, affords me all the opportunities I need to grow as an apprentice of Jesus (to learn patience, kindness, and so on) and to lovingly serve the people and tasks of my actual current life—just as it is.

Turning Toward Home

So far we've discovered the way temptation works and what won't work to get victory over it. Now it is time to unveil the historic and proven methods employed by apprentices of Jesus in the battle with temptation. The road we take next has as its name something old-fashioned sounding: *holiness*. But you will learn not to be afraid of it. You will see the practical goodness of it and how it is built into a person in nongrandiose, honest ways. Commands to holiness are frequent in the New Testament:

> Just as he who called you is holy, so be holy in all you do; for it is written: "Be holy, because I am holy." (1 Peter 1:15, 16)

> Make every effort . . . to be holy. (Hebrews 12:14)

> You are God's children. He sent Christ Jesus to save us and to make us wise, acceptable, and holy. (1 Corinthians 1:30 CEV)

But if all that talk about holiness worries you, perhaps *virtue* is an easier word to get your head around. Virtue is character based. An apprentice of Jesus, looking for the Way, constantly asks, who should I be? When we think of dealing with temptation in terms of virtue, we mean to appeal to the divine imprint on our lives. With virtue we are appealing to or adjusting our state of being, our character, habits, and readiness to act, desire, or feel.

The ancient practices for creating virtue that can defeat sin can help you become a new kind of person. They require the exercise of judgment, done peacefully and without drawing attention to ourselves, wherein we ask the question, What kind of person am I becoming through my interpersonal relations and the events, actions, and decisions of my normal days?

In the chapters that follow, ancient and fruitful means of grace await us, as well as practices through which we learn that Christian spirituality does not involve simply *trying harder* with old tools, as if we believed the hammer could ever remove the screw. Rather, the ancient practices you are about to learn have to do with *training smarter*. Maybe, for the first time in your life, you are about to be delivered from the tyranny of your disordered desires.

Ancient and Fruitful Practice

This warmhearted prayer comes from "A Prayer in Brokenness" from *Celtic Daily Prayer*. I use it when times are tough for some reason. After reading the last chapter, you may be feeling remorse over past sins or for using poor methods for dealing with temptation. Let this prayer cleanse and refresh you.

I ask you humbly, and from the bottom of my heart:

Please, God, would You write straight with my crooked lines?

Out of the serious mistakes of my life will You make something beautiful for You?[12]

TEN

ANCIENT AND FRUITFUL, PART 1

The two main enemies of the spiritual life [are] anger and greed. They are the inner side of a secular life, the sour fruits of our worldly dependencies.

—HENRI NOUWEN[1]

I was an active kid—cutting my own path, you might say. By second grade I was known as a terror. I don't know, though, about the word *terror*; it seems harsh. I was just having fun, and fun was paramount. I wanted my own way and was not about to follow the rigid demands of an early 1960s classroom, which seemed oppressive to the real inner me. One day the teacher grew weary of my fun. As punishment she told me I could not go out for morning recess. But she was stuck: she wanted to leave the classroom, and she didn't trust me to stay put as I was told.

The poor woman probably needed to go to the ladies'

room or get a cup of coffee. Now, forty-eight years later, I have pure pity for her. Frustrated by needing to go and not trusting me to stay, finally at her wit's end, she grabbed a roll of yarn and tied me to the chair next to her desk. She wound my legs, arms, and torso in yellow yarn, tying each part of me to the chair. And walked out!

Not one to tolerate having my path blocked, I knocked myself over sideways, scooted like an injured snake around to the front of the desk, and managed—I can't remember how—to get a pair of scissors and cut myself out. I have no memory of what happened next. But I knew well my next steps: the path to the vice principal's office. That, I am ashamed to say, is a totally true story!

If you've read this far in the book, you know we cannot be guided, as my second grade antics illustrate, by desire alone. Though some desires are good and others are neutral, unless we engage with the Christian spiritual transformation of our thoughts, feelings, will, and social self, we are not going to get far. We need a new path.

This new path is not something we need to create. It is not like the local government deciding to build an outer belt around your city. This path is ancient. It has been traversed for nearly two thousand years. For instance, in Egypt there is a monastery that has been in constant use for approximately seventeen hundred years. It is named after its founder, the revered father of the church, Saint Anthony. The paths from the outbuildings, which housed the sleeping quarters, to the church and the commons for eating are, as you can imagine, as well worn as are the paths around the monastery, which was used for prayer.

Imagine the vibe walking in those holy footsteps. Now, here is some really good news: that vibe was not created by hundreds of years of compressed dirt. The vibe came from what is rightly called Christian spirituality: the appropriately practiced spiritual disciplines that join human hearts and wills to the heart of God. Thus those paths are available to us in New York City and Bar Harbor, Maine; in Baltimore and the Outer Banks of North Carolina; in Atlanta, Georgia, and the Florida Keys; in Chicago and Houston; in Denver and Albuquerque; in Seattle, Portland, San Francisco, Los Angeles, and San Diego. The path of ancient, transformative practices can be created anywhere in America, anywhere in the world. These paths do not tie us up, cramp our style, or bind us. They are the true and good paths for finding the right inner stance for defeating temptation.

The Right Stance Through Ancient Paths

The first disciples and apprentices of Jesus in the Bible and the ancient, historic masters of the Christian faith knew that fruitfulness begins on the inside. But of course they were simply mimicking their master, Jesus. Jesus spoke of the inner DNA of a tree determining its fruit, of the inside of the tomb being the important thing, not how clean the outside was. Jesus also said it was abnormal to clean the outside of a cup but leave the inside untouched.

This is why one's inner disposition is so important when it comes to temptation. I want to dig a little deeper into our inner stance as we begin our work with ancient practices.

Working with historic forms of pursuing Christian formation will be the focus of the remaining chapters of this book.

I did not make up the idea that the inner position of our hearts, wills, and minds determines how we handle our desires. I learned it from contemporary masters in Christian spiritual formation. But actually it is a Jesus idea, one he passed on to his earliest followers and they then shared with those who came later. It is Jesus who said that it is not things exterior to us—temptations like chocolate or naked bodies—that defile us. We are defiled from within.

It is worth pausing for a moment to rehear the words of Jesus in their context. Jesus, travelling with his first followers, received some religious leaders as visitors. These leaders of Israel criticized Jesus for not keeping Jewish ceremonial laws. To which Jesus replied:

> "These people honor me with their lips, but their hearts are far from me. They worship me in vain; their teachings are merely human rules."
>
> Jesus called the crowd to him and said, "Listen and understand. What goes into someone's mouth does not defile them, but what comes out of their mouth, that is what defiles them."
>
> Then the disciples came to him and asked, "Do you know that the Pharisees were offended when they heard this?" . . .
>
> "Are you still so dull?" Jesus asked them. "Don't you see that whatever enters the mouth goes into the stomach and then out of the body? But the things that come out

of a person's mouth come from the heart, and these defile them. *For out of the heart come evil thoughts—murder, adultery, sexual immorality, theft, false testimony, slander.* These are what defile a person; but eating with unwashed hands does not defile them." (Matthew 15:8–12; 15–19, emphasis added)

James, the brother and follower of Jesus, had a first-row seat to these kinds of conversations. He clearly learned. He said, "Each person is tempted when they are dragged away by their own evil desire and enticed" (James 1:14).

The early fathers of the church understood the role of desire in this way too. For instance, a famous monk, Mark the Ascetic, started to answer a question from one spiritual seeker by saying, "You bewailed the fact that you are especially bothered by the passions of anger and lust . . . and you asked for words of encouragement about what sort of efforts and spiritual struggles you could make use of in order to position yourself above the aforementioned destructive passions."[2] Notice the words "position yourself." Mark then gives his inquirer some ascetic efforts to reshape his interior evils.[3] Ascetic efforts are spiritual training exercises. They are to the spiritual life what running, stretching, and weight lifting are for athletes. For instance, Mark said:

Do not let your mind be taken prisoner by lust, and do not defile yourself inwardly by giving your assent to sexually impure thoughts . . . [rather] following apostolic teaching, struggle to put to death whatever is earthly

(Colossians 3:5) and any indication or stirring of [inap-propriate] sexual passion.[4]

Mark gave that kind of spiritual direction because he knew, as do all spiritual masters in the Jesus tradition, that "the soul is led to slaughter by the fires enkindled by bodily pleasures, and the mind is taken prisoner by the seething heat of evil desire."[5]

If the fruitful practices for facing temptation are ancient, what path do we need to travel to get there? We will start with *solitude*, which, as we walk the path slowly, becomes *silence*. Soon enough, down the path, we find ourselves at a new des-tination marked by a welcome and wonderful reality: being no longer dominated by our desires.

Solitude

A core spiritual practice for any effective plan to gain vic-tory over temptation is solitude and its partner, silence. Without solitude we remain victims, for, as Henri Nouwen says, "Solitude is the place of the great struggle and the great encounter—the struggle against the *compulsions* of the false self, and the encounter with the living God who offers himself as the substance of the new self."[6]

In solitude others are not around to speak their words, so we can hear only two voices. One voice contains the inner shouts of our worries and anxieties and the clamoring din of desire. The other voice we hear is the loving, reordering, and reorienting voice of God.

Solitude rightly practiced moves from being a physical separation from the people and events of your life to being a spiritual reality and a groundedness. I've come to value these words from Nouwen as both instruction and a vision for the good life: solitude as a "quality of heart and an inner disposition"[7] that one experiences not just when alone, but *within* the rhythms and routines of one's actual life. This experience of heart-solitude, this encounter with the living Jesus, has the effect Jesus predicted:

> On the final and climactic day of the Feast, Jesus took his stand. He cried out, "If anyone thirsts, let him come to me and drink. *Rivers of living water will brim and spill out of the depths of anyone who believes in me this way*, just as the Scripture says." (He said this in regard to the Spirit, whom those who believed in him were about to receive. The Spirit had not yet been given because Jesus had not yet been glorified.) (John 7:37 MSG, emphasis added)

Connecting with Jesus through solitude creates a space, a reality within us from which flow gushing torrents of living water. This living water is usually made visible by acts of hospitality, service, power, and generosity. These acts embody and demonstrate the compelling vision of the apostle Paul: that life in the kingdom of God is "righteousness, peace and joy in the Holy Spirit" (Romans 14:17). Solitude, the bond it forms with Jesus, is *that* powerful.

But it is also self-authenticating. You have to try it to know it. You won't learn the experience from this book. You have to experience it on your own, the way a child no longer looks at the ground as a crawler but now sees the horizon as a walking toddler.

Silence

Could your mom whistle? Could you hear her voice down the block? Try to remember: You are going about the serious business of childhood play when you hear the voice or the whistle. Just then you stretch your arms across the chests of your friends to stop all movement. You hold your finger across your lips to shush them. And there it is again: the unmistakable voice, the distinct whistle calling you; no matter how far you've gone away, no matter what you may have been doing, there is the voice calling you back home. This is the purpose of silence: to shush noise, to pause life, and to hear God's voice, to hear him calling you back home, back to relationship, back to partnership, and back to your place in his story.

So now we are at the bend in the road where solitude turns to silence. As I write this paragraph it occurs to me that some readers may have been wondering where one could get the kind of knowledge of self that could contribute to defeating the lies and deceptions of temptation. Maybe you've wondered how to actually know your heart, your true inner system of desire. You are not alone in wondering such a thing. Jeremiah had the same thought and some insight to go along with it: "The heart is hopelessly dark and deceitful, a puzzle that no one can figure out. But I, God, search the heart and examine the mind. I get to the heart of the human. I get to the root of things. I treat them as they really are, not as they pretend to be" (Jeremiah 17:9 MSG).

Jesus, who is the Light of the World, can see into "hopelessly dark" places. The Spirit, too, searches us and reveals what is true about us. Solitude and its partner silence are two fundamental sources of such self-knowledge. They accomplish this on two levels. First, in silence and solitude I am made more aware, more conscious of what is currently real about me. Second, this new level of alertness carries over into the upcoming events of my life. Think of it this way: silence and solitude have direct and immediate spiritual benefits, and they make me more alert to my heart as daily life unfolds. This new alertness is golden in the spiritual life. With it we have potential and hope to make better decisions when tempted. Without it we are adrift, tossed by the wind and the waves. Self-knowledge leads to the appropriate self-control and thus appropriate actions. Darkness and self-ignorance leave us controlled by the various forces of life.

But finding solitude and silence is a challenge because my life often feels like it is made up of noise and words. I teach and write in many different roles: professor, author, pastor, bishop, and public speaker. I sometimes, literally, get weary of the sound of my own words. A little voice in me says, "Please shut up! Stop talking!"

But it is not just *my* thoughts and expressions. Words are everywhere. We live in a word-saturated world. Look around right now where you are sitting. How many sources of words are there? How many devices are there around you to make sounds of one kind or another? The God-created spiritual aspect of humankind was not designed to live in constant, word-filled noise. It is like asking a bird that has been drenched in oil to live well. Birds cannot, and do not, thrive in coastal oil spills. Humans cannot endure being covered in words and saturated in noise. From time to time we've got to take the path to solitude and then soak in silence.

Silence completes and intensifies solitude; it guards the fire within; it teaches us to speak.[8] From experience I know this to be true. I speak best when the speech emerges from silence. And I don't just mean the professional speech attached to the roles I listed above. I mean that my words to my wife, children, and colleagues are best when they are born of silence. This is true because, as Nouwen explains, "Silence is primarily a quality of the heart that leads to ever growing [love]."[9]

Silence is not just the absence of human voices, not just the stilling of the sounds of nature or the shushing of the noise of our industrialized world. Silence is the presence of God. In silence we hear the voice of God. Silence is not valued because it is superspiritual in the way a marathon runner who breaks the world record is superhuman. None of us can relate to that kind of feat. Silence has other reasons for its esteem: chiefly its power to rearrange the human self in the direction of godliness.

Through silence, apprentices of Jesus learn to be alert to their will, to what they really want and why they want it. By the practice of solitude and silence, we become aware that there is pressure, prodding, and pulling on our will by our thoughts, our feelings, and our peers. In silence we are given the clarity of mind and the strength of will to redirect our desires to the good, to God.

Without engaging in these core spiritual practices, we are adrift, like an oil-soaked bird, too burdened, too weary to even lift a wing. We have come to the place where we cannot change our position even if we wanted to. These are the points in life where the wisdom of Jesus and the historic practices of the church call out to us: Solitude! Silence! Wash off the commotion and clamor of life so you can fly!

Solitude and silence are the foundational, mainstay practices for putting desire in its place. They remind us that we don't *have* to have what we want. They give us hope—even assurance—that we can be delivered from the tyranny of what we want. Silence and solitude are like a prophylactic: they keep desire, flattered and enticed, from giving birth to sin; and sin, when of age, from giving birth to death.

Lady Desire and Lord Temptation: Giving Birth to Sin

I want to make a bold assertion here: I think James, the brother and close observer of Jesus, has the best handle on temptation of any of the writers of the New Testament. He conveys ancient and fruitful truths to deal with temptation. But I could be just speaking out of grateful enthusiasm. And you don't have to agree with me to take leaps forward in understanding temptation based on two sentences from the New Testament letter of James.

Over the past few weeks, as I've been writing this particular section—during Lent by the way—I have carried in my pocket a small piece of paper with a verse from James written on it. As I've memorized it and marinated in it, I've come to think that if all I knew about desire, temptation, and sin came from James 1:13–15, I'd be in decent shape:

> When tempted, no one should say, "God is tempting me." For God cannot be tempted by evil, nor does he tempt anyone; but each person is tempted when they are dragged away by their own evil desire and enticed. Then, after desire has conceived, it gives birth to sin; and sin, when it is full-grown, gives birth to death.

The backdrop for this passage is the tendency of God's people to blame him for their temptations. Why, we often wonder, did he give us desires for intimacy, nourishment, and security and then blame us for seeking sex, food, and money? Or, why did God give the law when he knew we could not keep it? But according to Dietrich Bonhoeffer, James is teaching us that "since evil has no place in God, not even the possibility of evil, temptation to evil must never be laid at God's door. God himself tempts no one. *The source of temptation lies in my own self . . . the place in which all temptation originates is my evil desires.* My own longing for pleasure, and my fear of suffering, entice me."[10]

There is more than the testimony of Jesus and James. Genesis 8:21 tells us that "every inclination of the human heart is evil from childhood." *The Message* puts it: "I know they have this bent toward evil from an early age." The *Amplified Bible* says: "The imagination (the strong desire) of man's heart is evil and wicked from his youth." The *New*

American Standard translates the verse: "The intent of man's heart is evil from his youth." Finally, the *Contemporary English Version* says: "All of them have evil thoughts from the time they are young." We are in trouble, but not because God has let us down, as the original readers of James thought. Disordered desire within us is the culprit.

James tells us that desire "gives birth" to sin. Really? Who then, is the second party to this pregnancy? Lord Temptation, that's who. He helps us to entertain and be entertained by wrong desires. He teaches us to treasure and take pleasure in them. Switching metaphors, once his hook is set in our mouth, in our desire, it is easy to reel us into sin.

But there is more: sin gives birth too. It gives birth to death. Spiritual death, one might say, is the grandchild of evil, lustful, or wrong desires. Like water from a storm-swollen river behind a dam, disordered desire, growing constantly from the downpour of temptation, busts out sooner or later and gives birth to a flood, sweeping men and women away to their deaths.

James is, again, wise about this. He instructs us that quarrels, fights, coveting, and killing come from *desiring* what we don't have (James 4:1–2). James's goal is to make it clear that followers of Jesus should not point to and blame external sources for temptation (especially God!), but rather recognize that we are lured and enticed by desires and passions that exist within us previous to external stimuli and without any outside help. One way to picture what James seems to have in mind is this: a fish is swimming along in a straight course and then is drawn off course by his appetite toward something that seems attractive, only to discover that the bait has a deadly hook in it.[11]

This is a hugely important insight. When we are tempted, it feels as though something in us is reaching out to obtain some thing or some experience. James, the observant brother of Jesus, in all his brilliance and Spirit-enablement, is shining a bright light on what is really true. An astute commentator shows us how this *reaching* eventually makes us the *reached-for*:

> When we reach out to satisfy disordered desire, we are no longer the seeking predator. We become the prey. It is we, who having crossed a dreadful line into the gun-sight of an expert hunter (The Devil), are at that time in danger. We are the one about to be shot, captured and imprisoned.[12]

James's spiritual insights are intended to produce clarity about the sort of life one intends to live. They ask us to make a decision: Will you follow the disordered desires of your heart, leading to death, or will you follow Christ, leading to eternal life? In his letter to the Romans, Paul, like James, boldly pronounced a similar choice: "If our minds are ruled by our desires, we will die. But if our minds are ruled by the Spirit, we will have life and peace" (Romans 8:6 CEV).

We've already established in an earlier chapter that we cannot simply jettison desire. We need it to pursue good, to pursue God. Rather, desire must be subordinated to what is good, and it is the role of the *will* to see to it that this happens. But the will cannot be left alone to fight the battle of temptation. The will can exert its power only if, by thoughts and feelings, by memories and positive social pressure, it understands what is good and is then bent and oriented toward the good, bent in the direction of God.

To get there, we've got to do a little more work discovering ancient and fruitful ways of dealing with temptation. In the chapter ahead we will do work with spiritual preparation, seeking first the kingdom of God and then bringing the whole human person into alignment with God—both with the goal of bringing that powerful synergy to bear upon desire and temptation.

Ancient and Fruitful Practice

This short prayer from the Great Litany in the *Book of Common Prayer* works well with solitude and silence. Sit with it in silence, interacting with the Holy Spirit based upon it. Ask, "how am I wired in inordinate ways?" Ask to be shown your sinful affections. Then ask for deliverance.

From all inordinate and sinful affections; and from all the deceits of the world, the flesh, and the devil . . . Good Lord, deliver us.[13]

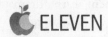 ELEVEN

ANCIENT AND FRUITFUL, PART 2

It is not hard to find the will of God.
The hard part is wanting to find it.
—WILLIAM C. SPOHN[1]

Temptations almost always come wrapped in some sort of lie or deception. The fraud provides the alleged reason we should give in to the temptation. Deception funds and supports the activity of temptation. Do you remember walking from the parking lot to your college classroom or job site and answering the Monday-morning question posed by a high school or college friend: "Did you go to the party Saturday night?" I have distinct memories that the parties rarely, if ever, lived up to the hype. And even the best party was soon forgotten. The disappointing parties of our youth are a valuable analogy for desire: we want something, we get it, and soon the thrill is gone. Then we want more, different, and better things. That is a dead end of the worst, most painful kind. But there is another way.

We are intended to find human fulfillment in the drama that is playing out as the kingdom of God, inaugurated in the coming of Jesus, moves toward final fulfillment. You and I were meant to live and move and have our being within that unfolding story. Following cravings, without first properly ordering our desires around the present and coming kingdom, will guarantee a life of restless searching. It can be no other way. Fulfillment outside the kingdom cannot be found because it does not exist.

The ancient Christians knew that unchecked desire could malevolently draw our attention to the wrong things. Recognizing what captures our attention is crucial because whatever that thing or person is, it has the capacity to put us completely under its domination. It is not just that these attention-grabbing allurements cause us to engage in acts of sin. It is that we become slaves to them. Our heart, the center of our being, and the core components of our whole personality come under the control of misplaced, disordered desire. "When that happens," says one scholarly diction-ary article, "all decisions of the will, and even the best and highest impulses and powers of [humans] are determined by these desires."[2]

What is the opposite of this oppression? What vision can we grasp and shoot for that can deliver us from this bondage? It is Jesus. It is life in the kingdom of God as he expressed and announced it. How do we get in on it? You do the things

necessary—grace-enabled spiritual disciplines of some sort—
to turn your life toward God. This is repentance. You align
your inner and outer life with the teaching of Jesus (see John
5 in *The Message*), and you make yourself subject to the story
of God. You then begin to act within its plot lines and character outlines by asking the Holy Spirit to fill you with the will
and capacity to do so.

The Historic Pattern

From the earliest days of the church, the understanding of
temptation is that it can be successfully dealt with.[3] My long-
time reading of the New Testament says to me that Peter,
James, John, and Paul did not walk around in any sort of
lasting fear, defeat, guilt, or shame, despite moments of weakness or failure. Neither were they naive, ignorant, or gullible.
They understood temptation from hard personal experience.
They saw the devil at work with their own eyes. But they also
watched Jesus command Satan to stand down with a word. If
we would experience the same sort of victory that Christians
throughout the ages have experienced, we need to follow the
approach detailed below.

We first begin by preparing for temptation now, before
it's upon us. When the opportunity to fall comes, we want
to be ready to stand and do the right thing. This can only
happen through the grace-enabled creation of inner goodness
and heart commitments made and strengthened by spiritual
training and preparation. If we are used to falling because
we've made innumerable compromises beforehand, we can

learn to strengthen our stand if we ready our hearts and minds before the attack of the enemy.

Some preparatory moves are thoroughly practical. Consider the thoughtful restraint of your social self and the physical places that you do or do not permit yourself to be in. Because "bad company corrupts good character" (1 Corinthians 15:33), there are some people I will not let influence my moral or spiritual life. I prepare a way ahead of time to be loving, kind, and generous, but not so connected that I am pulled into a spiritually harmful relationship. As there are, roughly speaking, *sacred* places such as churches and chapels, there are, roughly speaking, *wicked* places where ungodly influences hold sway. If at all possible, unless specifically called by God otherwise, I stay away from the harmful places. I do so with the prayer Jesus taught us on my lips: "Lead me not into temptation" (Matthew 6:13); lead me not into a space, sphere, or relationship in which I am out of my league but in the league of the devil.

Other preparatory moves occupy a more spiritual space, such as consciously reordering desires as a matter of practice. Ask yourself if you are loading your desires with, as Tim Keller says in *Counterfeit Gods*, "all the deepest needs of [your] heart for significance and transcendence."[4] If so, by working with the Spirit within your heart, you can intentionally and purposefully reevaluate and reorient your desires to fit God's order and plan. This isn't simply determining beforehand not to fall into sin, a determination that many of us have made to no effect. Rather, it is allowing and aiding the Spirit to reshape your wants away from sinful behavior.

Through such preparation we can grow in the capacity and intention to resist temptation. This is done through the well-thought-out, well-planned, intelligent, grace-based, Spirit-empowered use of the Christian spiritual disciplines. These include, in the Catholic, Anglican, and Orthodox parts of the church, sacraments such as baptism, Eucharist, and the Daily Offices. Other communities such as the Reformed and evangelical communities stress Bible reading and study, Christian fellowship, accountability, and prayer. These means of grace are all necessary and helpful tools for our battle with temptation, principally because God uses them to transform our hearts.

From the desert fathers to the modern movement of spiritual formation, the means of grace have been divided into two main categories: *disciplines of engagement* (such as worship, study, and prayer) and *disciplines of abstinence* (such as fasting, solitude, and silence). If I forced myself to give a basic and workable list, I would be happy to follow John Wesley: sincere prayer in all its forms, times, and places; diligent Bible study from the smallest word to the largest sweeps of the biblical story; and Eucharist, regularly participating in communion with a body of believers who are also employing the means of grace to grow in God and service to others.

We need these means of grace to reshape us because reacting in the moment as we are doing now is insufficient. Follow the story in chapter 14 of Mark's gospel to see more fully what I mean:

> They went to a place called Gethsemane, and Jesus said
> to his disciples, "Sit here while I pray." He took Peter,

James and John along with him, and he began to be deeply distressed and troubled. "My soul is overwhelmed with sorrow to the point of death," he said to them. *"Stay here and keep watch."* . . .

Then he returned to his disciples and found them sleeping. "Simon," he said to Peter, "are you asleep? *Couldn't you keep watch for one hour?* Watch and pray so that you will not fall into temptation. *The spirit is willing, but the flesh is weak."* (Mark 14:32–34, 37–38, emphasis added)

This is why we prepare and train through the wise and judicious use of Christian disciplines. We are mindful, and, to use Jesus' word, we watch. We don't count on our flesh "getting it" any better than did Peter, James, and John. We stay alert and get ready beforehand so that we are willing and able to trust and obey Jesus.

Seek First the Kingdom

When temptation is the topic, there is no ancient practice more powerful than seeking first the kingdom of God. Jesus taught his first followers to do so. But how do you do that if you don't really *want* to? You can't, at least not for long. To really seek something *first* implies by definition a reshuffling of one's desires. If one particular thing is going to be first, that means other things are going to be demoted to second, third, and fourth. I know how this works in practice.

A few years ago, when I had time for playing golf regularly, I learned that there is a *kingdom of Golf*, as well as the kingdom of God. As I got really into golf, I would, hearing Golf's kingdom calling, experience multiple yearnings during the workday to go to the local golf shop to try out various kinds of golf gear—drivers, putters, gloves, bags, clothes, shoes, and GPS systems—the works. I loved the smell of the shop. I liked trying new clubs in the demo area. I didn't have to strive or become a golf legalist to have these experiences. It felt like it just came to me, like the most natural thing in the world. In fact it felt so intuitive, so biological, that I imagined it to be involuntary like the beating of my heart. I was like the proverbial moth drawn to the flame or like my dogs drawn to the scent of the raccoons that live in the storm drains in front of our house.

Seeking first the kingdom of God is the oldest and most powerful way to put desire in its place and thereby nullify, for the most part, temptation. But as we've been discussing, this requires on our part continual grace-enabled repentance in order to align our thoughts, emotions, attitudes, and desires to match the character and nature of God's kingdom. Not in general, but specifically regarding temptation, what would it mean to put God's kingdom first—and his righteousness?

What kind of righteousness are we talking about when we talk about God's righteousness? What does it mean to seek it? What would such a life look like? Chiefly what is in view here is a way of life. *Covenant* is the all-purpose, all-encompassing term to describe this God-with-humans cooperative relationship. When speaking specifically about God's part of the relationship, covenant alerts us to God's initiating, consistent, active, forgiving love; his faithfulness, mercy, and grace.

On our side of the covenant, as God's people, the idea of covenant makes us attentive to the fact that we, as God's cooperative friends, have a mark, a target, a bull's-eye to joyously (not grudgingly or for merit) aim at—something like making par in golf. When our shots miss the target, or *miss the mark* (a primary biblical notion of sin), we realign, we repent.

When you live life in this manner, you will find that all the other needs and appropriate desires of life are taken care of, just as Jesus said (Matthew 6:33). It means all disordered desires are put in their place so that they no longer dominate our budgets, calendars, thought-life, and emotional health. *Seek first the kingdom of God*; nothing else, no plan, no strategy or tactic has power quite like it to rearrange, reorient, and reorder your desires.

The language above is a bit theological. Let's work with it a bit. What is the "kingdom of God"? Simply, it is the places and spaces where God's will is the reality, where all things are in perfect accord with his plans. Heaven is obviously such a place, as the Lord's Prayer instructs. What does it mean to seek it? It means to cultivate an inner desire for God and his kingdom. Dallas Willard and a group of mentors in spiritual formation give us this helpful guidance for such cultivation:

> "And you will seek me and find me," the prophetic word is,
> "when you search for me with all you heart." (Jer. 29:13)
> And again: "He is a rewarder of them that diligently seek
> him." (Heb. 11:6) This seeking is driven by the desire to
> be inwardly pure before God, to be wholly for him, to love
> him with all our heart, soul, mind and strength. Inseparable

from that desire is the desire to be good as Christ himself is good: to love our relatives, friends and neighbors as he loves them, and to serve them with the powers of God's Kingdom.

This seeking is implemented through the discovery of the state of our own heart and inner world by study, reflection, prayer and counsel; and then through the taking of appropriate measures to change what is not right within, as well as in the visible, social world of which we are a part. We find what God is doing in us and in the visible world and merge our actions into his. This is what Jesus described as "constantly seeking the kingdom of God and his kind of righteousness." (Matthew 6:33)[5]

Before we turn to the final chapters, let's spend a few moments thinking about these words from Peter and how they tie into the last couple of chapters:

Don't lose a minute in building on what you've been given, complementing your basic faith with good character, spiritual understanding, alert discipline, passionate patience, reverent wonder, warm friendliness, and generous love, each dimension fitting into and developing the others. With these qualities active and growing in your lives . . . no day will pass without its reward as you mature in your experience of our Master Jesus. Without these qualities you can't see what's right before you, oblivious that your old sinful life has been wiped off the books. (1 Peter 1:5–9 MSG)

These words assist my growth in Christ in two ways. First, Peter guides me into what to *do*. He shows me how to build on the initiation of God. Second, these words provide a vision for the kind of spiritual life actually available in our present, contemporary lives—maturing in Jesus with the old sinful life, not just the sins wiped away, but the bent to sin straightened as well. They alert me to the genuine possibility of growth in the spiritual life and a *reward* that comes, in this life, to those who find *the good life* in following Jesus, not in the fulfillment of disordered desire. Last, I find Peter to be exactly right: when I do not engage with God in the complementary, cooperative ways Peter suggests, I lose sight of everything that is right, true, and good about God, me, and the people and events of my life.

Ancient and Fruitful Practice

The prayer below is from the *Book of Common Prayer*. It is called a "Collect for the Renewal of Life." Pray it a couple of times. Focus on the words "drive far from us wrong desires" and the prayer to "incline our hearts" toward training in godliness. Go as slowly as you need to go to let your heart catch up to your mind.

O God, the King eternal, whose light divides the day from the night and turns the shadow of death into the morning: Drive far from us all wrong desires, incline our hearts to keep your law, and guide our feet into the way of peace; that, having done your will with cheerfulness while it was day, we may, when night comes, rejoice to give you thanks; through Jesus Christ our Lord. Amen.[6]

 TWELVE

LITURGICAL PRAYERS AND OFFICES

The liturgy and its Community: "They are not only on the way, The Way is in them."
—WILLIAM C. SPOHN[1]

If you, like me, have any experience with temptation, this prayer might be tailor-made for you:

> *Almighty and most merciful Father; we have erred, and*
> *strayed from thy ways like lost sheep. We have followed too*
> *much the devices and desires of our own hearts. We have*
> *offended against thy holy laws. We have left undone those*
> *things which we ought to have done; And we have done those*
> *things which we ought not to have done; And there is no*
> *health in us. But thou, O Lord, have mercy upon us, miser-*
> *able offenders. Spare thou those, O God, who confess their*

faults. Restore thou those who are penitent; According to thy promises declared unto mankind in Christ Jesus our Lord. And grant, O most merciful Father, for his sake; That we may hereafter live a godly, righteous, and sober life, To the glory of thy holy Name. Amen.[2]

That prayer, taken from the *Book of Common Prayer*, is called "a general confession." It is a useful introduction to liturgical prayer. But keep in mind that liturgy cannot be reduced to the Prayer of Confession. I don't intend to do that here, but I must say that perhaps because of all the sin in my life, I currently find this prayer the most moving part of Anglican worship.

This could also be the case because, as I am a newish Anglican bishop, Eucharist still makes me a bit nervous; it's high-gravity stuff if you take it seriously. But with confession? I am right there, concretely grounded in knowledge of myself, both yester*years* and yester*day*. Thus I sense the presence and work of the Holy Spirit every time I get on my knees in the midst of my community of faith and confess. The discernment of the Spirit's work only intensifies as I rise to my feet, lift my hands, and pronounce over my friends the grace-alone fact that we are all fully, amazingly, graciously forgiven:

Almighty God have mercy on you, forgive you all your sins through our Lord Jesus Christ; may he strengthen you in all goodness, and by the power of the Holy Spirit keep you in eternal life. Amen.[3]

Prayer and the Power to Transform

Before we look at the specific practices of liturgical prayer, I want first to tell you why there is a chapter on prayer in a book about temptation.

Prayer—interaction with God—is at bottom the only hope for dealing with temptation. But according to Henri Nouwen, "the crisis of our prayer life is that our mind may be filled with ideas of God while our heart remains far from him."[4] Ideas about God, standing on their own, are not normally transformative at the level of desire or the will; mere information never could be. Thus Nouwen says we need to "strive to let prayer remodel the whole of [our] person."[5] Liturgical prayers and practices, engaged with active and faith-filled participation, will reorder one's desires, thoughts, feelings, and will.

The amount of pertinent material in the *Book of Common Prayer* is too extensive to cover in a single chapter. Thus we need a way to select, focus, and structure the material. For our purposes here, we'll unpack the older Prayer of Confession as a way to introduce the power of liturgy to shape a life of victory over temptation.

It is entirely possible to engage in religious activities such as liturgy unspiritually and thus without real edification. If we do so, they will not liberate us from *the tyranny of what I want*. Be aware: it's what you intend to do with these prayers that is difference making. You must intend spiritual transformation. If you do intend it, you will find that God will be there waiting for you, providing all you need for your transformation.

As Nouwen suggested above, in prayer we seek more than knowledge about God. We strive for more than a grasp of true statements about God, as important as those are. But it is not nearly enough to know that *the Lord is my shepherd* as a bit of data or as a Scripture location—Psalm 23:1. Nor is it enough to know it as an analogy of God, and thus a deeper insight into the manner in which he cares—like a shepherd. These kinds of knowing are fine. There is nothing intrinsically wrong with them. They just don't go far enough. As Nouwen says, in prayer we want to come to an "inner experience of God's shepherding action in whatever we think, say or do."[6] That kind of knowing includes our brains but cannot be reduced to it. That kind of experiential knowing has the power to restructure the tyranny of disordered desires.

A major, blessed outcome of liturgical prayers is their power to pull us out of the unexamined, chaotic patterns of our daily lives and into a holy rhythm. Liturgy does this primarily through its vocabulary. The vocabulary of liturgical prayers is not taken from the street. It is taken from the sanctuary. This may throw you off a bit at first, but stick with it. You've got plenty of street in your life already—let a little sanctuary seep in.

Still not convinced? How's the street working for you now? If you can say, "just fine," then you might want to pass this book to a friend in need. If it's not working for you, then follow me into the sanctuary of liturgical praying.

The purpose of liturgy is to create virtue, a particular kind of virtue that worships and glorifies the one true God. We are not talking virtue in the cheesy sense of surface-only religion. We are talking virtue in the sense of a human life that is marked by good qualities, wholly alive and fully human as God intended: spiritually, emotionally, intellectually, and socially. It means becoming a person who, because of his or her manner of being, is a valuable asset to God and his or her community.

I will introduce you to the various bits of liturgy I use to specifically help me with disordered desire, temptation, and sin. I'll show you how I tend to use liturgy as a tool for transformation. Importantly, I do not ultimately trust in liturgy. I trust God, who meets me in times of liturgical prayer, public or private, silent or spoken. Just as importantly, I bookend my days by saying prayers—morning prayer and compline (evening prayers said just before going to bed). But these do not constitute the whole edifice of my prayer life. They are just the basics, the concrete foundation, the giant pillars on which moment-by-moment prayer is built. Throughout the day I also borrow from the prayers and exercises below to keep me present to the people and events of my life and alert to the voice and movements of God.

Under the headings below, based on an outline of the Prayer of Confession, here are several of the things that run through my mind during the day to fill in between the opening and closing prayers.

I Have Erred . . .

Anytime during the day that I can feel my heart slipping, I've got this reorienting prayer from the Great Litany (a comprehensive order for prayer) from the *Book of Common Prayer*: *"From all evil and wickedness; from sin; from the crafts and assaults of the devil; and from everlasting damnation . . . Good Lord, deliver us."[7]*

I Have Strayed from Thy Ways . . .

Again, when I can sense my attitudes, my patience, and my generosity of spirit waning, the Great Litany comes through:

> *From all blindness of heart; from pride, vainglory, and hypocrisy; from envy, hatred, and malice; and from all want of charity . . . Good Lord, deliver us.[8]*

> *From all false doctrine, heresy, and schism; from hardness of heart, and contempt of thy Word and commandment, Good Lord, deliver us.[9]*

I have used the prayer manual *Celtic Daily Prayer (CDP)* for personal use in the morning and evening for almost a decade. Its vocabulary and rhythms have really penetrated over the years. Listen to the capacity of *CDP*'s Morning Prayer of Blessing to call us home from straying hearts and begin the day in peace:

> *May the peace of the Lord Christ go with you, wherever he may send you.*
> *May he guide you through the wilderness, protect you through the storm.*

May he bring you home rejoicing at the wonders he has
  shown you.
May he bring you home rejoicing once again into
  [your] doors.[10]

I Have Followed Too Much . . .

Lent is a great time in the church calendar for spiritual transformation. Below is the collect (a corporate prayer said in
church) from the *Book of Common Prayer* for the fifth Sunday
in Lent. I suggested it as prayerful practice at the end of
chapter 3:

> *Almighty God, you alone can bring into order the unruly*
> *wills and affections of sinners: Grant your people grace to*
> *love what you command and desire what you promise; that,*
> *among the swift and varied changes of the world, our hearts*
> *may surely there be fixed where true joys are to be found;*
> *through Jesus Christ our Lord, who lives and reigns with you*
> *and the Holy Spirit, one God, now and for ever. Amen.*[11]

I don't know about you, but I do know about me, so I'll
just talk about Todd Hunter: given the intensity, the pace,
and the fullness of my life (and the swift and varied changes
of the world), I follow the devices and desires of my heart
way too much. But in this prayer I am reminded that in God,
by the Spirit, my heart and desires can be reordered, that my
heart may surely be fixed upon God and his kingdom, that
place where true joys are to be found.

I also make use of this line from the Great Litany (*BCP*): "*From all inordinate and sinful affections; and from all the deceits of the world, the flesh and the devil. Good Lord, Deliver us.*"[12]

The Midday Canticle from *CDP* is also a powerful antidote against following too much the devices and desires of a disordered heart:

> *Teach us dear Lord, to number our days;*
> *that we may apply our hearts unto wisdom*
> *Oh, satisfy us early with your mercy . . .*
> *Let the beauty of the Lord our God be upon us;*
> *and establish the work of our hands . . .*[13]

I Have Offended Thy Holy Laws . . .

Sometimes before the week is even in full swing, I am aware that I have offended the good sense of God found in his commands and decrees. But by bedtime on Monday, I am brought back to good thinking and to a good heart by these lines in compline (*CDP*):

> *Living God of the universe—may the Light of Lights come to my dark heart from Thy place; may the Spirit's wisdom come to my heart's tablet from my Savior.*[14]

> *Circle me, Lord, keep protection near and danger afar . . .*
> *Circle me, Lord, keep peace within; keep evil out.*[15]

By the time the workweek is over, come bedtime on Friday, these words from compline are on my lips, crying out against the devices and disordered desires of my inner man:

> *Lighten my darkness, Lord. Let the light of your presence dispel the shadows of night.*[16]

I Have Left Undone . . . I Have Done

When I become aware of what I have committed and omitted in order to sin, I have a ready-at-hand way to make a clean breast of it. In addition to the Prayer of Confession cited in full above, in *CDP* there is what has become for me an often used, well-appreciated Prayer in Brokenness:

> *I ask you humbly, and from the bottom of my heart:*
> *Please, God, would You write straight with my*
>   *crooked lines?*
> *Out of the serious mistakes of my life will You make*
>   *something beautiful for You?*[17]

There Is No Health in Me . . .

This phrase pulls no punches. It hits you in the face. I think of it often in contrast with Jesus, who, full of divine health, said of Satan that though Satan was *the ruler of the world, he has nothing in me* (John 14:30). We cannot get to Jesus' perfection. In this life there will always be pockets of dark in us, places where the enemy still has a foothold. Thus from the litany in the *BCP*, I pray:

> *From all inordinate and sinful affections; and from all the deceits of the world, the flesh, and the devil . . . Good Lord, deliver us.*[18]

From the *BCP* prayer for compline I ask God to:

> *Visit this place, O Lord, and drive far from it all snares of the enemy; let your holy angels dwell with us to preserve us in peace; and let your blessing be upon us always; through Jesus Christ our Lord. Amen.*[19]

And last, from the Evening Prayer in *CDP*, there are these Expressions of Faith and a section from the Prayer of Blessing:

> *Lord, you have always given peace for the coming day; and though of anxious heart, today I believe . . .* [20]

> *Lord, you have always kept me safe in trials; and now, tried as I am, today I believe . . .* [21]

Have Mercy on Us

When asking for God to have mercy on me, I think often of this Collect of the Day, called a Collect for Grace (*BCP*):

Lord God, almighty and everlasting Father, you have brought us in safety to this new day: Preserve us with your mighty power, that we may not fall into sin, nor be overcome by adversity; and in all we do, direct us to the fulfilling of your purpose; through Jesus Christ our Lord. Amen.[22]

I sometimes use this from the Great Litany: *"That it may please thee to give to all people increase of grace to hear and receive thy Word, and to bring forth the fruits of the Spirit . . . We beseech thee to hear us, good Lord."*[23]

And I sometimes recite this, from Sunday Compline (*CDP*), which I, being alone at bedtime, put in the first person to make it more concrete:

Be my light in the darkness
Be my hope in distress
Be my calm in anxiety
Be my strength in weakness
Be my comfort in pain

This, from *CDP*, is one of my most used, most experienced, and most beloved lines of liturgical prayer: *"The peace of all peace be mine this night . . ."*[24]

Monday Compline from *CDP* encourages me to ask for the mercy of God with these words: *"Into your hands I commit my spirit; I give it to you with all the love of my heart . . ."*[25]

Lastly, the compline for Thursday (*CDP*), guides us to God's mercy, which in turn leads us to God's peace:

> *Find rest, O my soul, in God alone: my hope comes*
> *from him.*[26]

> *Sleep, O sleep in the calm of each calm.*
> *Sleep, O sleep in the guidance of all guidance.*
> *Sleep, O sleep in the love of all loves.*[27]

We Confess Our Faults . . .

When it comes to confessing our sins, you can't go wrong with the Prayer of Confession I introduced at the start of this chapter. We Anglicans (other Christian groups have something similar) also have the Collect for Purity, which we say every week in worship. But you don't have to wait for Sunday morning to use it to get right with God. A priest doesn't have to say it for you. Consult it as much as you like. Better yet, memorize it as a moment-by-moment way to keep short accounts with God:

> *Almighty God, to you all hearts are open, all desires known,*
> *and from you no secrets are hid: Cleanse the thoughts of our*
> *hearts by the inspiration of your Holy Spirit, that we may*
> *perfectly love you, and worthily magnify your holy Name;*
> *through Christ our Lord. Amen.*[28]

Restore Us

When I think of liturgical prayer that beckons me in the direction of laying down pride and stubbornness, restoring me to proper humility and consciousness of my place in God's story, I think of this Collect of the Day (*BCP*). It is called a Collect for the Renewal of Life:

> *O God, the King eternal, whose light divides the day from the night and turns the shadow of death into the morning: Drive far from us all wrong desires, incline our hearts to keep your law, and guide our feet into the way of peace; that, having done your will with cheerfulness while it was day, we may, when night comes, rejoice to give you thanks; through Jesus Christ our Lord. Amen.*[29]

From the Great Litany there is this prayer of restoration:

> *That it may please thee to bring into the way of*
> *truth all such as have erred, and are deceived,*
> *We beseech thee to hear us, good Lord.*
> *That it may please thee to give us a heart to love*
> *and fear thee, and diligently to live after thy*
> *commandments,*
> *We beseech thee to hear us, good Lord.*[30]

When feeling a bit disconnected from God at the end of a busy day, I am always glad to see these lines from Tuesday and Wednesday Compline (*CDP*). They cry out for restoration with God:

> *Calm me, O Lord, as you stilled the storm.*
> *Still me, O Lord, keep me from harm.*

> *Let all the tumult within me cease,*
> *Enfold me, Lord, in your peace.*[31]

> *The peace of God be over me to shelter me, under me to uphold*
> *me, about me to protect me, behind me to direct me, ever with*
> *me to save me.*[32]

That We Might Live a Godly Life . . .

It's likely due to my temperament and personality, but I feel the most connected to this last petition—the prayer for a godly life. I like keeping things positive. And this last phrase from the Prayer of Confession surely leaves us with positive hope. In addition I make use of this prayer from the Great Litany (*BCP*). It moves me in the direction of repentance and of amending my life:

> *That it may please thee to give us true repentance; to forgive*
> *us all our sins, negligences, and ignorances; and to endue us*
> *with the grace of thy Holy Spirit to amend our lives according*
> *to thy holy Word,*
> > *We beseech thee to hear us, good Lord.*[33]

From *Celtic Daily Prayer*, I also make use of these excerpts from Morning Prayer. They provide for me focused intentionality and active participation for moving in a godly direction:

> *One thing I have asked . . . this is what I seek: that I may*
> *dwell in the [presence] of the Lord all the days of my life . . .*

to behold the beauty of the Lord [in all the people and events of my life].[34]

I also love praying the following prayer every morning. I never tire of it. It is my prayer for the conscious presence of God throughout my day. And I've discovered there is nothing more temptation smashing than the conscious presence of God. Think about it this way. You're a teenager, and a youth leader says this to you: do whatever you want in the backseat of the car—just first pretend that Jesus is with you. You're an adult: lie on your taxes or to your boss—just first pretend Jesus is with you. This isn't like a picture of Jesus you can just take off the wall when you want to sin in the room; I'm talking about a real conscious awareness that God is present with you, indwelling and surrounding you. Wanting to walk in the conscious presence of Jesus, I adore these lines from Morning Prayer (*CDP*):

> *Christ, as a light, illumine and guide me.*
> *Christ, as a shield, overshadow me.*
> *Christ under me; Christ over me*
> *Christ beside me on my left and my right.*
>
> *This day be within and without me, lowly and meek*
> *   yet all powerful.*
> *Be in the heart of each to whom I speak;*
> *In the mouth of each who speaks unto me.*[35]

These, too, for Saturday Compline (*CDP*) have a similar power:

> *May God shield me;*
> *may God fill me;*
> *may God keep me;*
> *may God watch me;*
> *may God bring me this night*
> *to the nearness of his love.*[36]

There you have it—a basic introduction to dealing with temptation through liturgical prayer. For roughly seventeen hundred years, millions of Christians from all over the world, from every tribe, nation, and language have used these liturgical prayers to defeat temptation and to grow in Christlikeness. Liturgical prayers do indeed, as the last line proclaims, bring us *to the nearness of his love*. But there is more nearness, more power, more love and intimacy to be had. This is found in the divine immediacy of Sacraments.

Ancient and Fruitful Practice

This chapter is full of practices. You've been exposed to a lot of spiritual tools. Now let's use this simple prayer of dedication. When I use it at bedtime, I actually move my arm from my head to my toes as I say it. Try it a few times—dedicate your whole self to God.

From the crown of my head, O Trinity, to the soles of my feet mine offering be.[37]

 THIRTEEN

SACRAMENT:
GOD IS WITH US

*Whom have I in heaven but you? And earth
has nothing I desire besides you.*
—PSALM 73:25

It was September 1968 in my hometown, Santa Ana,
California. My seventh-grade French teacher was a really
lovely lady. She deserved more respectful students than me.
One afternoon, as she was calling class to order, I, having not
taken my seat as asked, was loitering against the back wall
finishing a conversation with someone who was just then
heading to his seat as ordered. When she noticed that I was
not moving, my teacher called to me in the French name she
had assigned me the first day of class: Jacques.

"Jacques," I heard her sweet, French-accented voice call.
"Sit down, *s'il vous plaît.*"

Since I couldn't tell her where I wanted her to go in French, I did the next best thing. Like a frustrated tourist in Paris, I used hand signals. I used *the* hand signal, the mother of all one-fingered hand signs. Yep, I did it. I told her, accompanied with swear words, that I was not going to sit down, *merci beaucoup!*

Had I been paying attention to anything beyond my apparently angry heart, that would have been a teachable moment. I say *apparently* because I still don't know why I did these sorts of horrible things to teachers. Nevertheless, having merely received more swats from the vice principal, I missed the opportunity to have learned a vital lesson about how the reality of the spiritual world is conveyed in the reality of human life.

The lesson I missed then, but have learned in hindsight, is that the unseen evil world, both the one in my heart and the one managed by Satan, can convey its malevolence through the material world: even through material things as little as a middle finger or a tongue. But I was several decades from understanding that God conveys himself through material, sacramental means as well.

What Is a Sacrament?

I realize that some people reading this book are not veterans of the liturgical and sacramental world. But hang in there; you will be able to easily grasp the goal of this chapter, which is to answer this question: How does receiving the sacraments build in us the kind of life wherein we appropriately order our desires and find a story so life compelling that temptation is no longer tempting?

But before we get there, for the sake of those outside sacramental churches, let's give a workable definition of the term *sacrament*. The basic definition in most liturgical churches is that a sacrament is an outward and visible sign of an inward and invisible reality. Further, a sacrament conveys something real. It communicates the grace of God to which it points or signifies. We'll say more about this below, but for now keep in mind this simple pattern: baptism conveys new life in God; Eucharist makes real to us the intention of Jesus in the Upper Room that we would be nourished by him—by his body and blood.

For our purposes here, though there are thousands of volumes written on the meaning of sacrament, we do not need to go deeper than this: instead of thinking of heaven and earth as always and everywhere separated by a cosmic brick wall, think of them as intertwining or overlapping. God's realm, though wholly different by his wise and sovereign choosing, touches our realm. Peter and Paul saw life-changing visions, Moses heard the voice of God from a burning bush, and the apostles cast out demons after the pattern of Jesus.

These few examples, and hundreds more from the Scriptures and millions more from the two-thousand-year life of the church, demonstrate that the sphere of God intersects with our sphere whenever God wants the overlap to happen— and that is a lot more often than some of us would think. So, at least with regard to the sacraments of baptism and Eucharist, just imagine God's realm breaking into ours and conveying his goodness to us.

Most importantly for our discussion on desire and temptation, as William C. Spohn says, "Scripture makes it clear that trusting faith and faithful practice are the avenues 'to know the Lord.' There is a knowledge that comes only from participation, from living inside the circle of faith . . . even an inconsistent participant understands a way of life better than the most fair-minded spectator."[1] Baptism and Eucharist get us off the sidelines, out of the bleachers, and into the game. From this new vantage point there is experiential knowledge available that one cannot get from anywhere else. This knowledge, like knowing rules to a new board game, allows us to play against disordered desire and win more often than we might be currently.

The Role of Sacraments in Defeating Temptation

The sacraments we will consider here, baptism and Eucharist (holy Communion), give us the outline of the Christian story. Baptism reminds us we needed to be born again. Participation in Eucharist teaches us that there is an infinite spiritual resource available to Christians through participation in the life of Jesus and death of Jesus as experienced in Eucharist.

Without the story that baptism and Eucharist tell us, there would be no motivation to deal with desire. If our sense of story had to do only with getting our desires fulfilled, we would have no reason, and thus no hope, to deal with wrong desire. But, as those who think closely about worship teach us, "when you take upon yourself the symbols of baptism and the Lord's Supper, you are saying, 'I am part of the people over whom the Lord Jesus Christ is sovereign.'"[2] Beginning with our ancient Christian forefathers and continuing up to today, baptism has been the sign that someone is a follower of Jesus within the community of faith, both universal and local. Such a person then sustains a life of followership through the Eucharistic meal Jesus has been hosting for his people for two thousand years.

Baptism

Let's first consider baptism as a rich source of power for defeating temptation. At baptism the dying and rising of Jesus happens to us as well. We go under the water in death and rise from it to identify with Jesus, to take on his life, to join up, to publicly declare allegiance to Jesus, and to enter into the new covenantal partnership with God. Coming through the water, we are delivered from bondage and set in a new reality of freedom.

That is the story in which "I don't have to have what I want" makes sense. I don't know of any other story that can carry that load. Next, having been delivered by this story from the "tyranny of what I want," I can then begin to look at my interior life. Without this deliverance I cannot do so—I am in bondage to my desires. Remember: before we surrender to God in baptism, in spite of appearances to the contrary, we are the hunted, the prey, not the hunters.

Through baptism a whole new reality emerges. In our new life in Jesus, desire comes back to the table. Earlier in the book I said that we could not just throw desire out, that we need desire. Now you can see why: we need desire to pursue the good of our new life. The Bible gives us a good look at this new interaction with, and reprioritizing of, desire:

- "I desire to do your will, my God; your law is within my heart." (Psalm 40:8)
- "What the righteous desire will be granted." (Proverbs 10:24)
- "The desires of the diligent are fully satisfied." (Proverbs 13:4)

According to Spohn, the Christian story, as outlined by baptism and Eucharist, is vitally important because "who we understand our selves to be and how we interpret what is going on will determine what we think we ought to do."[3] Our new story becomes the interpretive grid for all of life: sexual, economic, family, social relationships, work, play, and so on. Thus, Spohn says, "When Christian individuals and communities try to figure out what to do . . . they should do so in reference to who they are called to be as disciples of Jesus Christ."[4]

The baptismal vows of the Christian church are very similar across denominations. For our purpose here, I have selected a few of the vows we Anglicans, using the *Book of Common Prayer*, take in baptism. I do so as a way to place before your imagination the power of baptism to conquer sinful desire, temptation, and sin. Think through these questions and answers as a force against temptation:

Q: Do you renounce Satan and all the spiritual forces of wickedness that rebel against God?

A: I renounce them.

Q: Do you renounce the evil powers of this world which corrupt and destroy the creatures of God?

A: I renounce them.

Q: Do you renounce all sinful desires that draw you from the love of God?

A: I renounce them.

Q: Do you turn to Jesus Christ and accept Him as your Savior?

A: I do.

Q: Do you put your whole trust in His grace and love?

A: I do.

Q: Do you promise to follow and obey Him as your Lord?

A: I do.[5]

In summary, then, we can say this: Baptism draws together all the threads of the biblical story, all the chief ends of God: creation, fall, election, sin, exile, exodus, and finally the new and permanent exodus achieved in Jesus and enabled by the power of the Holy Spirit. In baptism we say two things: "this is my story" and "this—the worldwide and local version of the church—is the community in which I will live it out."

Eucharist adds even further dimensions to the biblical story.

Eucharist (Holy Communion)

Eucharist teaches us to abide in and find our life in "the Vine." You can probably recall the famous words from John, chapter 15: "I am the vine, you are the branches." I want to show you a portion of this passage from *The Message* with the hope that it will begin to cast a vision for Eucharist as a way to abide in the Vine, a way to deal with temptation:

> Live in me. Make your home in me just as I do in you . . .
> When you're joined with me and I with you, the relation
> intimate and organic, the harvest is sure to be abundant.
> Separated, you can't produce a thing. (John 15:4–5 MSG)

Making our home in Jesus through weekly participation in Eucharist is like cosmic weed killer and fertilizer blended into just the right formula for a great, green and healthy spiritual life. The weed killer gets rid of unwanted growth and clears our mind, making room for rightly ordered desire. The fertilizer in it nourishes us and stimulates spiritual growth.

This abiding, this connected participation, this giving and receiving of love during Eucharist, allows a way of knowing that is available nowhere else. It is a rich, deeply respectful, worshipful, and profound participatory knowing that is rooted in committed love. Such knowing does not set aside or even challenge scientific knowing. It is like science is having one conversation in the parlor while Eucharist participation is having a completely different conversation in the dining room. Increasingly knowing Jesus through Eucharist is *unique* in the sense that there is nothing like it. But because Jesus instituted it two thousand years ago and because it has been practiced for all that time, it is not *odd*. Most importantly, we need this unique knowing of Jesus to assist us in freeing ourselves from the tyranny of disordered desire.

You have to *know* something in this experiential sense we've been talking about above to put desire in its place. When asked what exactly we should *know*, I commend the biblical story from which Christianity has emerged. Granted, there have been, and are, Christians with inappropriate structures of desire, but hundreds of millions of Christians have experienced radical transformation of their inner selves, including desire, by immersing their whole lives in Jesus, in his kingdom story. Don't let the visible exceptions deceive you. There is power in Jesus to realign desire, thus rendering most temptation obsolete.

Let me show you next, through an outline of some highlights from a Eucharistic worship service, how I have nurtured an imagination for the power of Eucharist. The prayers below are taken from the *Book of Common Prayer*.

In Your Infinite Love

Every week I say the prayer below to God in the presence of, and on behalf of, my worshipping community. The words to this prayer give further insight into the worldview, the story, and the pattern that put desire in its place.

Holy and gracious Father: in your infinite love you made us for yourself, and, when we had fallen into sin and become subject to evil and death, you, in your mercy, sent Jesus Christ, your only and eternal Son, to share our human nature, to live and die as one of us, to reconcile us to you, the God and Father of all.[6]

This prayer reminds me every week that I don't own myself—including not owning my desires. I am made for God. I am a sinner. As such I have become subject to my desires, not master of them. But God in his mercy reversed the curse. He has put to rights my relationship with my Creator. He has made me free. Now I work with him to implement this victory into my life through the practices spelled out in this book.

The next Eucharistic prayer I want to highlight is this:

We celebrate the memorial of our redemption, O Father, in this sacrifice of praise and thanksgiving. Recalling [Jesus'] death, resurrection, and ascension, we offer you these gifts.

Sanctify them by your Holy Spirit to be for your people the Body and Blood of your Son, the holy food and drink of new and unending life in him. Sanctify us also that we may faithfully receive this holy Sacrament, and serve you in unity, constancy, and peace; and at the last day bring us with all your saints into the joy of your eternal kingdom.[7]

In this prayer I am asking God to make the bread and the wine be for us, and do for us, whatever it was, fully, that Jesus had in mind in the Upper Room. We ask with celebration because the life of Jesus has already begun in us. We recall Jesus and all the events of his life, including death, burial, resurrection, and ascension, and this becomes our story too. Remember our discussion of baptism above: we die under the water to our life and its desires, and we rise again with a new life and the agenda of that Christ-life.

We ask that as we obey Jesus' command in Eucharist, the story of redemption will sanctify us. In so asking, we are really saying, "God, set us apart for you, for others, and for what you are up to on the earth." I am passionate about the words *unity, constancy,* and *peace.* I linger on them in my heart every week. They mark for me the kind of life in which I would like to make meaning of my desires, of my life. These words remind me of my commitment to reorder my desires thusly: I want to live in unity with the whole church; I seek a life of constant followership of Jesus; and I want to be a person and agent of peace.

Next, so everyone can see them, I lift the bread and wine and say to my waiting community of faith: "The gifts of God for you, the people of God. Take them in remembrance that Christ died for you, and feed on him in your hearts by faith, with thanksgiving."

It is then time to feast on all the goodness and grace of God that is communicated to us in Jesus. These words inspire me to take my heart, will, mind, emotions, social self, and spirit and say yes to God with them. This declaration rouses me to use the Sunday instance of holy Communion to create an ongoing communion with God that others around me experience as for their good. That is to say that by eating and drinking goodness and grace myself, I become a carrier of goodness and grace to others.

Our last prayer is said all together; it is the Prayer of Thanksgiving:

> *Eternal God, heavenly Father, you have graciously accepted us as living members of your Son, our Savior Jesus Christ, and you have fed us with spiritual food in the Sacrament of his Body and Blood. Send us now into the world in peace, and grant us strength and courage to love and serve you with gladness and singleness of heart; through Christ our Lord. Amen.*[8]

These words are moving to me as I say them in church. I was not, however, prepared to be moved by them as I cut and pasted them into this book. The words "send us now into the world in peace" leap off the page of my Order for Worship every week. Having tasted and seen it, I have come to relish peace as a foundational part of the Good Life. When my peace tank is full, I have an easy time dealing with desire and temptation. Once anxiety kicks in, look out. I'm apt to be looking for, apt to desire, something to dull the negative emotion. Thankfully, I've got enough experience to know that fulfilling disordered desire is never the right or functional thing to do. It leads only to *less* peace.

Last, I highly value this final bit of Eucharistic praying: "And grant us strength and courage to love and serve you with gladness and singleness of heart."[9]

Singleness of heart speaks to rightly ordered desires. Our enemy knows this and strives, along with flesh and the world, to promote in us all the disorder and duplicity he can.

Writing this chapter, and the one before it on prayer, has brought some new awareness to me. Upon reflection, I can see I have been significantly shaped by my first two years of liturgical and sacramental practices as an Anglican rector and bishop. In my prior, low-church experience, I would have been sincerely afraid that all these prayers and practices were wooden, dry, and devoid of the work of the Spirit. I hear the same from friends who have not been on this side of the fence. Fair enough. I do not take it personally.

But for me, I've got to honestly testify that the historic practices of the church have proved to be fruitful indeed. They have seen me through two of the most adventurous and difficult years of my life.

Having been so blessed, I find myself loving to pronounce the benediction on our community of faith. In just the last few weeks of Lent 2011, I discovered and grew quite fond of the Prayer of Dismissal from the Australian *Book of Common*

Prayer. I commend it to you now as a summary of our work in sacraments and as a way to shape the story of our lives such that temptation is put in its place:

> *God who has called you is faithful.*
> *Go into the world with joy,*
> *forgive generously,*
> *love extravagantly,*
> *live abundantly.*
> *And the blessing of God,*
> *the Father, the Son and the Holy Spirit,*
> *be upon you now and forever. Amen.*[10]

Ancient and Fruitful Practice

After ten years of almost daily use, the lines from Morning Prayer in *Celtic Daily Prayer* below, have become real friends to me. They were first composed and prayed by Saint Patrick of Ireland. They are his famous "Lorica" or "Breastplate" prayer. Pray this prayer slowly, thinking of the sacramental aspect of each line. Consider how each line—a material thing—makes God present to you.

> *Christ, as a light, illumine and guide me.*
> *Christ, as a shield, overshadow me.*
> *Christ under me, Christ over me,*
> *Christ beside me on my left and my right.*[11]

 FOURTEEN

THE LECTIONARY: SEEING SIN IN CONTEXT

Saying no is possible—you may just need a reason to do so.

—AUTHOR

How many born-again Christians do you know who prayed the sinner's prayer at an altar and remain today, sometimes decades down the road, still caught up in a story that is anything but godly? If you simply pause right now and take a couple of deep breaths, several or many might come to mind. Sadly, even close friends and family members. Maybe you are even thinking about yourself.

The most common ancient antidote for dealing with a controlling narrative that leads us away from God is to switch stories, to take on a new story. This is very much at the center of what the word *repent* means. Repentance includes asking ourselves: What is the story in which we think we are living? Stories are powerful not least because they involve characters and an unfolding plot: a beginning, middle, and conclusion.

Repenting—switching stories—allows us, in the middle of life, before the conclusion, to find a new life, a new way of following Jesus, before the finale sneaks up on us, as death always does. Stories work the way I am suggesting because most of us have a story in our hearts. We have become a character in that story. The plot of that story is telling us what to do next. When we wonder, "Is *this* the right move?" the story has the answer.

When I was in the tenth grade, or sometime thereabout, I joined a drinking club called Early Times. It was named after a brand of Kentucky whiskey. We all wore hip-looking jackets that had an Early Times patch on it, designed by a founding member. I hated whiskey then, and my opinion hasn't changed since. I'm no fan of alcohol, but I needed to act my part in the cool and fun story I was telling about myself. I tried so hard to look cool in my Levi 501s, a new white T-shirt from JC Penney, and of course the jacket with my club patch. Early Times shaped the key plotline in my story, telling me and everyone else that I was cool and that I was having fun.

Frames, Boundaries, and Foundations

"We all tend to see in terms of what we know and believe," says Max De Pree, a Christian leader I admire.[1] Stories tell us what to know and what to believe. They become frames, boundaries, and foundations. These frames can either include or exclude the majority of temptations. When we choose God's story and seek alignment with it, these boundary markers hold up a large sign saying "No Temptation Allowed," even though a few always sneak in. Every building has a foundation. The foundation determines what can be built upon it. It doesn't take an engineer or a geometry teacher to tell us that you normally do not build a circular building on a rectangular slab of cement.

What is true of cement is true of our lives: we cannot build a life-with-God on a story of our own making, a story of life-according-to-my-desires. A life-with-God is unfailingly built upon his story. God's story gives us a vision by and purpose for which we can live. This is crucial to spiritual growth that defeats temptation because, as De Pree explains, "people without sight develop other abilities; [but] people without vision constantly struggle to find hope."[2] I have a suggestion for an effective vision regarding reordered desire and temptation. I have been working on it for years and can tell you it works. Here it is: I have been trying to become the kind of person who is, to use De Pree's description, "at ease with personal restraint . . . who welcomes constructive constraints and seeks simplicity" as an essential aspect and condition of holiness, thus arming my inner person for victory over temptation.[3] The ancient source for finding constructive constraints, boundaries, and frameworks is a story, an ancient text: the Bible.

In liturgical churches we read this story aloud every week. We read a passage from the Old Testament, a psalm, a section of an epistle from the New Testament, and a passage from one of the four gospels. For instance, this morning we read the story of the choosing and anointing of David as king over Israel; Psalm 23; a passage from Ephesians; and the story, in John chapter 9, of the healing of the man born blind. Carrying on in this fashion, in the space of one year we will have read aloud the central plot of the biblical story. Over a period of three years, we will have read aloud almost the whole Bible.

There is one thing this ancient practice does: it sets forth a story that beckons the whole world to enter. It asks us to make a choice: are you in that story or out? Our response to that story then sets the tone for our lives. Placing our lives in that story enlarges our capacity to defeat temptation; creating a story of our own diminishes it.

There is a very big difference between a commitment to "not sin" and a commitment to and devotion to God and his story. The former has no power to fundamentally reorder desire, but the latter does. Temptation of all kinds is defeated by broadening the view from which temptations come and looking at the solicitation to sin in the larger context of life and of God, seeing things as they really are, as we discussed previously. What is really in play here is the power of story to shape our imaginations and to keep us from escapism.

Let's think about the role of imagination first. In Christian circles imagination is often viewed with suspicion. Many people believe the word suggests a lack of concreteness and reality, that it can only mean untrue, fictional, fairy-tale, and of the mind as opposed to that which is real and existing outside the mind. But there is a positive, helpful, and good sense of the word too, and it is this meaning I have in mind when I suggest the usefulness of our imaginations in the process of spiritual formation. I mean this: imagination can mean the ability to form mental images; to place concepts before our minds; to find a way to make sense of and understand the world; to hold in our minds images of what is real, true, and good that correspond with and are consistent with reality.

Thus, with all genuine respect to those who have some fear regarding the word, I want to say plainly here that I do not believe one can follow Jesus without an imagination for what that might mean. Most human beings develop an imagination in the positive sense through story. "I am a mom" has a whole story attached to it that forms behaviors and attitudes. "I am a celebrity" does the same, as does "I am a professor," and so on. You need an imagination for following Jesus. I suggest you get it from reading and grasping the unfolding story of Scripture. To do this, you may need to stop reading the Bible as a dictionary or encyclopedia or religious tidbits. You may have to set aside reading it as a self-help book. Read it for what it means to be: a story that invites your participation in it through trusting and following Jesus, learning what it would mean to be a mom, a celebrity, or a professor from him. That one vital decision will move you solidly down the path of defeating temptation. And you know why by now: it will reorder your desires!

Let's now consider the power of story to ground us in reality and work against the need to escape from real life. A statistic from the Barna survey stands out to me: the second-most-cited reason respondents supplied for giving in to temptation was the desire to get away from their life as they were currently experiencing it. Escapism is always an effort to find relief from some horrible pressure one feels. Why is escaping such a motivation that we give in to sin? What is so bad about common life that we need to escape from it?

One way to understand our need for escape is to recognize that humans were made for big drama—to be the cooperative friends of God working his will in the world. When we don't live in the story, we get bored and need an escape into something—usually illicit things—that will entertain us, thus getting our minds off the boredom we so often feel. This is to say that escapism is born from and tied to our wrong desires as they stand in opposition to God and finding our place in his story.

Week after week as we read Scripture in church, we are called back to the only story in which we thrive, in which we make sense of life such that we no longer feel the need to escape it.

The Scriptural Narrative As the Norming Norm for Life

What has *norming* power in your life? What pulls your life together? What do you use to make sense of life? Whatever that default narrative is, you routinely act from it. If that statement is true and if you are losing a battle with temptation, maybe we should try to find a new "norming norm" for our lives.[4] As you would guess, I commend the story of God in the Bible as the norming norm for Christian life.

Reading the Bible in this way works. It is an ancient vehicle for being delivered from the tyranny of what you want.

Who we see Jesus to be as we read the stories of the Gospels and read the reflections of the apostles on Jesus in the epistles is meant to give us our basic moral compass, our ethical map. Now that you've seen how this works in public worship, let me now demonstrate how it can work in your personal life as well.

The Lectionary in Practice

Imagine you've come to church with me. As we approach the door, we are warmly welcomed. Entering the sanctuary, we become aware that there is a beautiful period of silence happening as a prelude to the remainder of the worship service. After some sung worship, the appointed readings for the day are read aloud in the manner I described above.

Now imagine that you are hearing the texts below read aloud. Your active participation during the readings is to *listen*. Don't just *hear*, but *listen* for the plotlines of your story, the one in which you have agreed to act. Below each text I will give you examples of how I interrelate with the text.

Darkened Hearts

The Epistle reading this morning is from Ephesians 4:17–19:

> So I tell you this, and insist on it in the Lord, that you must no longer live as the Gentiles do, in the futility of their thinking. They are darkened in their understanding and separated from the life of God because of the ignorance that is in them due to the hardening of their hearts. Having

lost all sensitivity, they have given themselves over to sen-
suality so as to indulge in every kind of impurity, and they
are full of greed.

What do you hear? I hear, "I need to switch stories" (*no
longer live as the Gentiles*). I hear, "I need to search myself"
(for any *futility of thinking* or *darkened understandings* about
life). I hear, "Where is God?" (Am I *separated* from him? Is
my *heart* hard?)

See how it works? We don't just read or hear the lectionary reading of the day—it reads us. The stories in the
lectionary readings illuminate our lives, interior and exterior.
They provide the possibility for weekly reordering of desire.

Carry on now in the same manner, reading the Scripture
passages below as if you were hearing them in church and
then considering my examples as a way to engage the text.
Use your best active reading and participate energetically. As
you read, consider the words of William C. Spohn: "Reading
scripture schools [our] affections . . . they tutor [our] basic
emotional tendencies."[5]

Desires Choke Life

Picture yourself sitting in church. Next in the order of worship is the reading of the Gospel. We all stand in worshipful
respect as the Gospel is walked into the midst of the community to be read. The Gospel reader begins by saying, "The
Holy Gospel of our Lord Jesus Christ according to Mark
[4:18–19]." The reader continues, "The seed is sown . . . but

the worries of this life, the deceitfulness of wealth and the desires for other things come in and choke the word, making it unfruitful." I participate in this text by silently, in the deepest considerations of my heart, asking myself, "Are my desires becoming disordered and thus choking the word and life of Christ in me?"

The Word of God Is Alive

Imagine this reading unfolding in church. "The Epistle reading for today is from Hebrews 4:12–13":

> For the word of God is alive and active. Sharper than any double-edged sword, it penetrates even to dividing soul and spirit, joints and marrow; it judges the thoughts and attitudes of the heart. Nothing in all creation is hidden from God's sight. Everything is uncovered and laid bare before the eyes of him to whom we must give account.

In this passage I hear hope—hope that Scripture can see (*nothing is hidden*) and reach the deepest parts (*soul and spirit*) of my heart to rearrange my thoughts, amend my attitudes, and modify my out-of-whack desires.

Put Off . . . Put On

How might you interact with this text if it were a part of the lectionary readings some Sunday? "The Epistle reading this morning is from Ephesians 4:20–24":

That, however, is not the way of life you learned when you heard about Christ and were taught in him in accordance with the truth that is in Jesus. You were taught, with regard to your former way of life, to put off your old self, which is being corrupted by its deceitful desires; to be made new in the attitude of your minds; and to put on the new self, created to be like God in true righteousness and holiness.

I interact with the text this way: I hear that it is possible, even likely, that followers of Jesus still have to deal with *deceitful desires* that *corrupt us*. I hear that a major aspect of spiritual transformation into Christlikeness, and thus a crucial component of defeating temptation, is to *put off our old selves* and *former ways of life*. Next I hear that, on the positive side, we are *to put on the new self* and that in so doing we will find substantial victory over temptation through *God's true righteousness and holiness*.

It is a wonderful thing to hear passages like that read, to hear them commented upon in a Scripture-respecting sermon, and then, after Eucharist, to walk out of the church into the world with a story and a hope that we can put off our old stories and put on the story of God. This happens when you follow the examples above: Don't just hear the Word; let it examine you. Interact with it. Don't just ask what a text *means*; ask what it is meant to *do* to you.

Futile Without a Story

In the perfection of the garden, Eve, though warned against it, saw that the fruit of the forbidden tree was good, pleasing, and desirable. So she took some, ate it, and then gave the forbidden fruit to Adam too. Contrast Eve's disordered desires and rebellious longings with the desires of Mary, the Mother of Jesus.

Whereas Eve lived in the perfection of the garden, Mary was asked to wrap her mind around the notion of a virgin giving birth. She had Joseph to worry about and her own reputation and that of her family to be concerned about. Mary lived in the dust of a confused and lost people. The chief characteristic of Mary's community was confusion and religious quarrels among the various religious bodies. This led to hatred that rivals the current political hatred we now have between conservatives and liberals in America. In Mary's day there was a lot of mean-spirited arguing going on about the correct way to be the people of God. In the midst of this disorienting cultural and religious mind-set, Mary, upon hearing from the angel, said: "I am the Lord's servant . . . May your word to me be fulfilled" (Luke 1:38).

Disordered desire was at home in Eve. Fundamentally, sinful desire cannot grow in the heart of a person like Mary. Anyone who can say, "I am the Lord's servant" and "Bring on your plan, God" will not have to worry much about defeating disordered desire or trouncing temptation.

With no sense of *out*, there is no solid feeling for *in*. With no knowledge of *up*, what can *down* mean? Temptation means little apart from the story from which it emerges. What is that story? It is the story of God. In the examples above I've tried to demonstrate how I use God's story to sort out my feelings, thoughts, desires, and intentions. If feeling A presents itself,

I place it against the backdrop of the story and let the story of God make meaning of my feelings rather than letting my feelings command and control my will. If thought B comes to mind, I set it also in the story and ask myself: Does this thought work well within God's story? Does it align with his intention for me as an actor within that story?

The sample texts we looked at got you started in the right direction with this practice. But it occurs to me that many readers may not come from a church background that produced in them a clear and succinct understanding of the biblical story. Let me tell you God's story in brief so you can pick it up as a way to understand a given verse, like the ones in this chapter, and as a way to sort out the impulses of your life.

The story began before creation, before space or time as we have come to know and experience them. It began within the triune reality of one God in three persons. The triune God, being a person, had intentionality before anyone saw that intention outwardly expressed in the sun, the moon, the earth, and the earth's swimming, walking, and flying creatures.

At the pinnacle of creation were women and men. The first man and the first woman were given special status as the cooperative friends of God. Sin entered the picture, and all the "it is good" of creation was shattered, fractured, and broken. God then began a cosmic re-creation and restoration effort. At the front line of that effort was the calling of Abraham and the creation through him of the people of Israel. This new, specially called people were to be God's servants on the earth, his friends, executing his plan to reclaim creation.

Israel famously failed in her vocation. God sent prophets, priests, and kings to pull his people back into alignment with the story, but to no avail. This frustrating pattern continued up to the time of John the Baptist. But with the coming of John, things began to shift. John prophesied that a new dawn—he called it the inbreaking of the kingdom of God—was emerging, that someone was coming after him who would be the Difference Maker in bringing this about.

Against all odds, against all biological realities, Jesus was born to a virgin, Mary. He apparently lived a normal childhood and became a man who worked with building materials. Soon everyone could see he was different. At first he seemed to be a prophet, but more. It was said of Jesus that no one, no rabbi, no prophet, had ever taught with his special kind of powerful authority. He seemed to be the wisest person ever. There was more. No one had ever seen the deeds of power Jesus accomplished. He stilled storms, raised the dead, and healed the sick. Demons even fled at his command.

Soon, however, various religious and governmental authorities grew worried about Jesus' power and influence over the common folk. Together they, along with a betraying insider, arranged to have Jesus arrested, tried, beaten, berated, mocked, and crucified. Several times, as this story unfolded, Jesus said that he was laying down his life and dying *for our sins*. For our forgiveness. For our regeneration. To reconcile us to him. To lovingly and graciously bring us back into *the story of God*.

More stunning than his virgin birth and his astonishing life was his *reaction* to death. Death could not hold him. The first Easter morning the tomb burst open with life: with

Jesus as the first of a new kind of humanity, with us in his death-defeating wake. Happily, joyfully, thankfully, there was no reasonable doubt about the resurrection of Jesus. He appeared to his friends and to five hundred more.

His first followers, the ones who captured and preserved for us his words and deeds, echoed these facts. But before they could go public with this news, Jesus told them to wait for the promise of the Father, for the ability they would be given to finally carry out the intention of God. Jesus, right before their eyes, then went back to the place from which he had come, to God and to God's sphere, to what we call *heaven*.

Not long after, while Jesus' friends were gathered together in a room, the promise was finally fulfilled. They were all filled with the power of the Holy Spirit. They were given power, authority, and gifts to carry out their vocation as the new people of God. The Spirit was released in them to begin the process of character transformation so that they would not fail, as their ancestors had. They were given new animation, new energy, and new orientation for all the various aspects of their lives.

It took me a few minutes to type that brief overview. It has taken me decades to learn to fit my thoughts, feelings, desires, intentions, and will into that story. But there is no other way to make meaning of my inner desires and the outer sources of temptation that come my way moment by moment.

It is no wonder we are living in futility, with extensive moral and ethical challenges. Having lost our story, we have no compelling reason to be moral or ethical. But now you know the story. You now have a worldview and framework through which you can sort your inner and outer realities. That is a huge step forward and away from futile attempts to deal with temptation.

Fasting Your Way into the Story

Thoughtful self-denial and reasoned self-restraint have always been at the heart of Christian spirituality. These two traits have often been wrongly viewed as mere goals. This wrong thought goes like this: *if I begin to fast or set aside other wants, I am, by that activity alone, a spiritual person.* Asceticism as a *means* to an end has fallen out of the popular vocabulary. In the biblical record, in the way of Jesus, abstinence is not just stopping certain activities such as eating food. It may surprise you to have this thought, but the *stopping*, the self-denial inherent in abstinence is meant to *start*, continue, and yield progress in the spiritual life. Its goal is to clear space and make room for something new. It is not emptying one's life for the sake of emptiness. Rather, it is like cleaning old mildewed food from the refrigerator in order to restock it with fresh, nutritious groceries. The biblical idea behind asceticism is *training or exercise into godliness.* The point is not the training; the point is godliness. The goal is not to exercise; the goal is to grow spiritually, nurtured by the exercise.

When I speak of asceticism I never have in mind extreme measures that would harm your body or harm the others in your sphere of influence. I always have in view small steps, one at a time, that slowly but surely over time rewire our hidden systems of desire. These small, ascetic deaths to our self reveal to us that we really do not have to have what we want. Often we can do better without it. But you'll never know this until you pick up the practice of self-denial as a means to loving God and your neighbor with ever-increasing depth.

This process and its outcomes are what Jesus had in view when he said, "If anyone desires to be My disciple, let him deny himself [disregard, lose sight of, and forget himself and his own interests] and take up his cross and follow Me [cleave steadfastly to Me, conform wholly to My example in living and, if need be, in dying, also]" (Matthew 16:24 AMPLIFIED BIBLE).

That lays it all out on the table! But how do we say no to our self in a culture that says unless you indulge your self you are a loser of the worst kind? How do we forget our self in a culture that says paying attention to our needs, wants, desires, and wishes is a really important thing to do? If we don't do this, we are sometimes warned, we will cease to exist as really in-tune, in-touch, with-it people. We need someone to give us a way to imagine how the kind of slow but sure *fastings* I describe above do in fact set us aside—and in so doing reveal a better person, more human as God intended, freed from the tyranny of what we want. Eugene Peterson is in my opinion characteristically brilliant in his treatment of these words of Jesus in *The Message* (Matthew 16:24–26):

> Then Jesus went to work on his disciples. "Anyone who intends to come with me has to let me lead. You're not in the driver's seat; I am. Don't run from suffering; embrace it. Follow me and I'll show you how. Self-help is no help

at all. Self-sacrifice is the way, my way, to finding yourself, your true self. What kind of deal is it to get everything you want but lose yourself? What could you ever trade your soul for?

What would you trade your soul for? Are you trading your soul for something right now? If so, can you stop the trading process? You can. The way there is to engage in proper, grace-enabled, sensible little acts of asceticism: little fastings, little deaths. Try it. Let someone else pick where to go to lunch tomorrow. Stop to listen to someone when you'd prefer five more minutes at the gym. You'll see that on the other side of the *little* death—giving up what you want—is a *large* resurrection of spiritual life!

Spiritual life is the vision and goal of dealing well with temptation. We sometimes fear the journey of getting to this new life because it calls for a letting go of what is known and comfortable. In the conclusion I'll give you a few tools to facilitate that new beginning.

Ancient and Fruitful Practice

This chapter highlighted the story of God and demonstrated how through the weekly readings of the lectionary we are weekly invited to enter that story. Below is a morning prayer drawn from Psalm 27:4, slightly edited by me to reflect the way I actually use it. This prayer always orients me to God and his story. Focus on the words *dwell* and *behold*, contemplating how Scripture facilitates these two actions in the people and events of our lives.

> *One thing I have asked . . . this is what I seek: that I may dwell in the [presence] of the Lord all the days of my life . . . to behold the beauty of the Lord [in all the people and events of my life].*

CONCLUSION
A NEW BEGINNING

The world and its desires pass away, but whoever does the will of God lives forever.

—1 JOHN 2:17

If you are struggling mightily against temptation and you've read this far, you surely are a focused and determined person. I respect and honor you! But in a few minutes it will be time to put this book down. If you're reading at bedtime, in a few short hours you'll have to acknowledge the morning and face the daylight signaling a new day with all its possibilities for sin and goodness. If the day has begun and you are reading on a train, bus, or subway, then today's meetings and toil are just a few stops ahead. If you are in your favorite reading spot, it won't be long until the phone rings or a child runs through the room. These settings and scenarios are gentle but cold-blooded and concrete reminders that temptation, sin, and victory exist around the clock, in the light of day and in the dark of night.

Coming now to the conclusion, I want to move from vision casting and information to some favorite tools for equipping you to face your disordered desires and temptations.

Tools You Can Carry: Hope

Let's get into the idea of hope by considering a confidence-building notion from Max De Pree. Writing about the holiness of leading people and shaping godly work environments, Max says: "Of what is hope composed? Certainly part of the answer is the ability to make choices—choices that set us apart and shape our legacy."[1]

Rather than feeling hopeful about the change, to come apart from the past and create a new legacy, I can make a well-educated guess about what many readers are thinking now: *My past haunts me. It strips me of confidence the way hurricane-force winds strip leaves from trees.* Previous fiascos dealing with temptation can seem to us like a pile of trash stretching all the way to the moon. But here's the deal, the undistorted fact regarding our past: it is either something that controls us, or it is the backdrop to a new story. To choose the first alternative is to have lost all hope.

Is it possible to change? Can we become someone different? Not without hope. Hope is the primary tool you must have on you at all times. We need hope that this time, no matter the past string of bad choices, we can begin the process of change. Sadly, hope is delicate. It is hard to get, and like a scared bunny, it is easy to run off. Hope is in short supply for those who have often battled temptation and lost. For them, hope is the last few pennies of what was once a full, sustaining jar of loose change. The death of hope will kill any possibility for dealing well with temptation. The death of hope, the inability to see a different future, is what makes people give up and give themselves completely over to desire.

If you battle with a lack of hope, go back to your favorite exercise at the end of one of the chapters. Find something you marked or underlined, something you tried and felt God with you as you did the exercise. Do the exercise again. Do it until it gives more hope. Then add another simple exercise that gives you similar hope. Hope doesn't just shrink—it also grows. Get on the growing edge by reconnecting to God's grace and his ability to transform us as we surrender our will to his.

Tools You Can Carry: Vision

Vision is very important to me. A preferable future, more fully devoted to Jesus, pulls me forward in my walk with him. An old hymn by Isaac Watts, whenever I sing it, helps to inspire this vision. These few lines are especially powerful in shaping my imagination for what it might mean to reorder my desires:

> *My richest gain I count but loss . . .*
> *and pour contempt on all my pride . . .*
> *all the vain things that charm me most . . .*

were [even] the whole realm of nature mine,
that were an offering far too small . . .
love so amazing, so divine,
demands my soul, my life, my all.[2]

Vision comes in two parts. The first part is your vision of what you do not want to occur in the future. The second part is your vision of the preferable future you want to bring about. If you need a little help visualizing the negative side of desire run amok, the thing you do not want to happen to you, consider Solomon:

> *I denied myself nothing my eyes desired*; I refused my heart no pleasure. My heart took delight in all my labor, and this was the reward for all my toil. Yet when I surveyed all that my hands had done and what I had toiled to achieve, everything was meaningless, a chasing after the wind; nothing was gained under the sun. (Ecclesiastes 2:10–11, emphasis added)

> God gives some people wealth, possessions, and honor so that they lack nothing their hearts *desire*, but God does not grant them the ability to enjoy them, and strangers enjoy them instead. This is meaningless, a grievous evil. (Ecclesiastes 6:2, emphasis added)

When I am tempted to let desire overtake my vision for the good, I think about Solomon. He beats us all, well at least most of us. Outside of the rumors one sees in the tabloids,

I've never known anyone who could actually say, "I deny myself nothing." Solomon went down the road of desire to its end—its bitter end, its go-to-the-sink-and-spit-it-out bitter end. By stuffing his face with more than he could enjoy, he made his life meaningless. I've never been the brightest bulb in the room, but I am practical. I do not need to learn lessons by experience that can be learned by the experience of others. Solomon, I have two things to say to you: I feel bad for you, and I thank you.

What about those who, unlike Solomon, *resist* temptation? Are their lives marked by emptiness and vanity? We alluded to it at the start of the book, but let's look more deeply again at the story of Joseph and Potiphar's wife. We pick up the story in Genesis, chapter 39: "Now Joseph had been taken down to Egypt . . . [and] the LORD was with Joseph so that he prospered" (vv. 1–2).

As you know, later the drama heats up as Joseph refuses the sexual advances of his boss's wife. We'll get to that. But here I want you to see that refusing inappropriate sex when offered is a result of prospering in the Lord. It is not a way of earning spiritual prosperity from God. Joseph could refuse because he was walking in a spiritually prosperous relationship with God. Hold to that vision: the vision of becoming, through the things we talked about in this book, the kind of person who would automatically, so to speak, do the right thing.

On the other hand, the inability to flee sexual sin will not bring the judgment of God; the inability is itself the judgment of God on a life thusly positioned. It is the result of a pattern of ignoring God. After some time God gives us over to ourselves, to our sinful desires, to our shameful lusts, to our depraved minds, and to our outright rejection of him (Romans 1). This is a frightful, dreadful position to be in. As Solomon, the expert on desire, put it, the lack of self-control leads to unpleasant results: "Like a city whose walls are broken through is a person who lacks self-control" (Proverbs 25:28).

But let's get back to Joseph:

> He lived in the house of his Egyptian master . . . Joseph found favor in his eyes . . . Potiphar put him in charge of his household, and he entrusted to his care everything he owned . . .
>
> Now Joseph was well-built and handsome, and after a while his master's wife took notice of Joseph and said, "Come to bed with me!"
>
> But *he refused*. "With me in charge," he told her, "my master does not concern himself with anything in the house; everything he owns he has entrusted to my care . . . How then could I do such a wicked thing and sin against God?" . . .
>
> One day he went into the house to attend to his duties, and none of the household servants was inside. She caught him by his cloak and said, "Come to bed with me!" But he left his cloak in her hand and ran out of the house. (Genesis 39:2–12, emphasis added)

How did Joseph refuse? Maybe the better question is, why did he refuse? We could have a quiz here, and most of you, having read this far, could give the right answer. The correct answer is powerful because it provides the vision that is a tool you can carry around: Joseph refused because his desires were rightly ordered. He wanted to please God, and Potiphar on behalf of God, more than he wanted to fulfill natural sexual desires.

We pick up the story when Potiphar's wife lies about Joseph, telling the other servants that he did in fact have sex with his boss's wife: "When his master heard the story his wife told him . . . he burned with anger . . . took him and put him in prison, the place where the king's prisoners were confined" (v. 19).

Am I the only one who, at this point, would be asking God, "Is this the reward I get for remaining sexually pure?" But Joseph, strongly oriented to God, always bent toward the vision of what God might be doing next—even in difficult and seemingly unfair circumstances—would have no part of such whining. In Joseph we see the biblical vision of an inner life, a structure of desire operating via the power of God. This kind of life not only avoids temptation but has a positive love to it, a self-giving love that brings to bear the kingdom of God on earth. You see it here and in the rest of Joseph's story:

> While Joseph was there in the prison, the LORD was with him; he showed him kindness and granted him favor in the eyes of the prison warden. So the warden put Joseph in charge of all those held in the prison, and he was made responsible for all that was done there. The warden paid no attention to anything under Joseph's care, because the LORD was with Joseph and gave him success in whatever he did. (vv. 20–22)

See the goodness that exists in the vision for a well-ordered life? It is good all around: for God, for us, and for others. As Screwtape instructs Wormwood, "When [God] talks of [Christians] losing their selves, He means only abandoning the clamor of self-will; once they have done that, He really gives them back all their personality, and boasts (I am afraid sincerely) that when they are wholly His they will be more themselves than ever."[3]

That is precisely what happened to Joseph. He lost himself in loving service to God and his boss and got back his life and more: he became a historic example of *humanity as God intended*.

In the six months I researched, thought about, and wrote this book, one vision, small but concrete, has stayed with me. I see some of it in the life of Joseph, but its finest, most perfect example is in Jesus. The setting for the vision is the Upper Room scene as described by the gospel of John. In the fourteenth chapter of John, Jesus is explaining to his first apprentices all that was going to unfold in what we now call Holy Week. He told them he was leaving but that he would leave them filled with peace and the power of the Holy Spirit. He then said that he would not be with them much longer because "the prince of the world is coming" (v. 30). Jesus then makes what is to me one of his most stunning remarks, and he seems to say it with complete, no-hype calm: "The prince of the world . . . has no hold over me."

That, frankly, has been my personal goal, in part for twenty years and in whole for the last six months. I know I'll never get there, but getting closer to *there* pleases the Lord.

It's good for my family, my work, and my colleagues in ministry—for anyone who has to interact with me.

I have also had it in the back of my mind every time I've talked about "well-ordered" or "disordered" desire. I have a feeling a few readers may have been saying, "Shut up already about desire!" Now, I hope, you can see why I've been banging on about it.

Joseph was free to refuse sexual advances precisely because of his well-ordered system of desires. Peter, denying Christ, was hopeless precisely because his stated desire—*sincerely* stated desire—not to turn his back on Jesus was in conflict with another desire to which he was more deeply committed. Safety? Fear of embarrassment?

Jesus of course knew this about Peter. Jesus could say of himself, "The prince of this world has no hold over me," but he could not say it about Peter. Jesus knew the opposite to be true. The cock, as Jesus predicted, did in fact crow upon Peter's third denial. But Jesus did not give up on Peter. Jesus will not give up on you. Hang with Jesus, through the ups and downs of temptation as Peter did—you'll be fine.

Tools You Can Carry: Plan Ahead

This perhaps could be called a coping skill, but I also think of it as a tool for managing temptation while we are in the midst of working on the inner person, of which desire is one part. The tool is this: plan ahead to stay out of places, situations, and relationships that you know are a mismatch for a godly system of desires. In the world of commerce and business, this is now known as "preloading a decision."[4]

With this tool I aim to give you a way to deal with peer pressure that matches a temptation to a sinful desire in you. *Switch*, a leadership book by Chip and Dan Heath, offers a helpful insight on this topic: "We all talk about the power of peer pressure, but 'pressure' may be overstating the case. Peer *perception* is plenty . . . [This is] rigorously supported by empirical research . . . You are doing things because you see your peers do them. It's not only your body-pierced teen who follows the crowd. It's you, too. Behavior is contagious."[5] The Bible has a point of view about this too: "Bad company corrupts good character" (1 Corinthians 15:33).

It was Peter, whom we just critiqued, who urged his readers, based on his experiences, "as aliens and strangers in the world, to abstain from sinful desires, which war against your soul" (1 Peter 2:11). *Abstain* here means, of course, "Don't do it!" but abstinence can also begin with "Stay out of those places!"

I also cherish the way the apostle Paul articulates a vision for planning ahead:

> That means you must not give sin a vote in the way you conduct your lives. Don't give it the time of day. Don't even run little errands that are connected with that old way of life. Throw yourselves wholeheartedly and full-time—remember, you've been raised from the dead!—into God's way of doing things. Sin can't tell you how to live. After all, you're not living under that old

tyranny any longer. You're living in the freedom of God. (Romans 6:12–14 MSG)

I like the idea that *sin can't tell me how to live*, that I am not *under that old tyranny any longer*. Carry the vision of such a reality in your mind. Use it as a way to plan for victory over temptation.

Tools You Can Carry: What's Working?

We, in every area of life, not just temptation, tend to obsess about what is wrong, why things are wrong, and how we might fix them. But this obsession steals the time and energy we need to examine more powerful and illuminating questions, such as *what's working?* And the corollary, how can I do more of that? Recall times in the past when you have triumphed over a moment's temptation; as Chip and Dan Heath put it, "find the bright spots" where the mercy and provision of God and planning ahead in terms of environment came together to produce victory over temptation.[6] If you are struggling with a temptation, sit with this kind of thinking for a while. Grow the good things that are happening with the goal of turning those good things into habits because, as the Heaths say, "habits are behavior autopilot."[7]

In time, avoiding temptation will substantially be autopilot for you. One of my big heroes in life, John Wooden, the famous basketball coach, said: "When you improve a little each day, eventually big things occur . . . [so] don't look for the quick, big improvement. Seek the small improvements one day at a time—that's the only way [progress] happens—and when that kind of progress happens, it lasts."[8] Having given you four tools to use in the battle with temptation, I now shift from *things* to *persons*. Jesus is on your side, and the Holy Spirit is beside you in the battle.

Jesus Is on Your Side

I know the doctrine of the inspiration of Scripture is important, and I have orthodox views about how Scripture came to be. But there is a time to talk about something in theory, and there is a time to use it. Firemen can explain all you want to know about water pressure in their fire hoses, but if you have a fire, you want them to use the hoses, not defend them or explain them. It is in that spirit that I cite the Scripture passages below. I want you to know that in your struggle against temptation, Jesus is an ally, a teacher, and leader on our side. The time will come for judgment, but as long as you are working to bend your inner structure of desire in a God-ward direction, that judgment is not for you.

Picture Jesus as your ally:

- "Because he himself suffered when he was tempted, he is able to help those who are being tempted." (Hebrews 2:18)
- "For we do not have a high priest who is unable to empathize with our weaknesses, but we have one who has been tempted in every way, just as we are— yet he did not sin." (Hebrews 4:15)

- "Therefore he is able to save completely those who come to God through him, because he always lives to intercede for them." (Hebrews 7:25)
- "The reason the Son of God appeared was to destroy the devil's work." (1 John 3:8)
- "I have told you these things, so that in me you may have peace. In this world you will have trouble. But take heart! I have overcome the world." (John 16:33)
- "You, dear children, are from God and have overcome them, because the one who is in you is greater than the one who is in the world." (1 John 4:4)
- "Simon, Simon, Satan has asked to sift all of you as wheat. But I have prayed for you, Simon, that your faith may not fail." (Luke 22:31–32)
- "My prayer is not that you take them out of the world but that you protect them from the evil one." (John 17:15–19)

Can you hear it? Do you get it? Jesus knows what you are going through in temptation. Jesus prays for you. He came, and comes to you, to protect you from the evil one, to destroy the devil's work. Become conscious of the reality that in your hour of trouble and temptation, you can receive his peace. Maybe the best promise of all regarding temptation comes from 1 John 4:4: "Greater is he (the triune God) that is in you than he (the evil one) that is in the world."

The Holy Spirit Is Beside You

I can recall some of my earliest New Testament Greek lessons. There was one in particular wherein we learned that the Holy Spirit is the one "who comes alongside us." Or that he is "the comforter." I've hung on to those notions for thirty-some years. But there is more. Concerning our topic, temptation, you and I also need to be *enfruited*. There is no real and sustainable progress in the spiritual life, including victory over temptation, without the fruit of the Spirit growing in our lives. The fruit of the Spirit is love, joy, peace, forbearance, kindness, goodness, faithfulness, gentleness, and self-control. Those attributes could also be called *the masters of sinful desire* or *the defeaters of temptation*. I find useful the way *The Message* sums up Paul's logic in Galatians 5:16: "My counsel is this: Live freely, animated and motivated by God's Spirit. Then you won't feed the compulsions of selfishness."

The preceding paragraph is not just a quick nod to the Holy Spirit. If you actually begin the journey this book commends, you will soon find that you need help. You may even begin to feel alone, like you are the only one "trying to be good." The psalmist, too, felt the lonely agony of such thinking. He said:

> But as for me, my feet had almost stumbled;
> My steps had nearly slipped.
> For I was envious of the boastful,
> When I saw the prosperity of the wicked.
> (Psalm 73:2–3 NKJV)

Thus the knowledge that God is with us on this journey is not just religious jargon. It is as vital to your spiritual life as your heart is to your physical life. Why? Because you are going to fail. But when you fail, God and his love for you will not. This knowledge will allow you the peace, confidence, and space to take the long view of defeating temptation. It will allow you to reject two common errors in the spiritual life: pride and fear. And be mindful of this: sometimes the Holy Spirit comes to you "with skin on" in the form of loving friends, anointed spiritual directors, patient pastors, and devoted counselors and mentors.

Just work with your transformation day by day, choose small doses of self-denial, accept small doses of divine affirmation, and be at peace with the growth such an approach brings. Remember: the world as God created it, the world as you currently experience it, is always safe for you—just as you are, without being perfect—not least because God, the creator of it, is with you in it by the Holy Spirit.

Let Him Do Anything but Act

It is time now to put our learning into action. Screwtape, telling Wormwood what to do if a Christian begins to repent, says, "The great thing is to prevent his doing anything. As long as he does not convert [repentance or resisting temptation] into action, it does not matter how much he thinks about this new repentance . . . Let him do anything but act. *No amount of piety in his imagination and affections will harm us if we can keep it out of his will.*"[9]

It's time now to engage our *will* in the new way we have learned in this book. That is, to get our heart, thoughts, feelings, and social self on board, pulling in the same direction. You will never triumph over a moment of temptation unless your spirit, heart, will, mind, thoughts, and feelings are acting as allies. This may sound like too much. You may think, *how am I supposed to be conscious of six inner, hidden aspects of myself when a beautiful person or an obvious time to lie presents itself?*

I can empathize. And actually I am not asking you to be self-conscious in that way. I am casting a vision for a transformation of life, through the power and grace of God, which is so complete that dealing well with temptation becomes rather automatic and subconscious. But our inner self is often like the chamber of the United States Senate: fully and firmly divided. Our thoughts and feelings often have major disagreements with each other. Then they each lobby the *will* to get their way. This is why, when starting a diet, we often get rid of everything in the cupboard we might crave in the coming days. We are using our brains to manage feelings that might come in the future.[10]

This sort of whole-life transformation, of course, commits us to apprenticing ourselves to Jesus. That, in turn, puts us on the path of Christian spiritual transformation. When desire rears its head, when temptation whistles for desire to come out to play, you are going to want to look down and see that your feet are firmly planted on the path of spiritual transformation into Christlikeness.

Pause with me here for one last brief moment: Think of a recent time when you had victory over sin. Next call to mind the biggest single victory over temptation you have ever had, like the time you said no to the amazingly stimulating affair or the huge financial incentive to lie on a report at work. Got that in mind? How did you manage on that occasion? I can tell you. Your heart, mind, thoughts, will, spirit, and feelings were pulling in the direction you decided to go, whether you were conscious of it or not.

The sort of spiritual growth we have in mind in these last couple of paragraphs is not a lot different from learning to dance or to swing a golf club properly. An instructor makes you conscious of errors, and you do it right—your mind and body cooperate—but the next time you go out to try it on the dance floor or the course, you get it wrong. You are made conscious again, get it right a second time, and then blow it again. On and on this circle of trial and error goes until at some point the right dance step or the correct swing becomes ingrained in your muscle memory.

Your heart, your will, and your spirit have the same capacity to learn, and they have learned some things as illustrated by the victories over temptation you called to mind a moment ago. In your hidden, inner self you have partial allies. But they sometimes slip into neutral or even get into cahoots with the enemy. In this book we have learned together how to work with God to further transform those inner elements into full-time, consistent allies.

Loving Desire, Desiring Love

In the incomparable wisdom of God, love is the fundamental organizing power in human life, if we'll work with it and not against it. Love, God's kind of love, is the model for and motivating force for putting desires in their proper place.

Jesus' final conversation with Peter in the twenty-first chapter of the gospel of John makes this clear. In verse fifteen and following, there is a conversation between Jesus and Peter. Jesus begins the dialog by asking Peter, "Do you love me?" Peter answers, "Yes, Lord, you know I love you." There is an obvious play on words happening in the Greek text of the New Testament that for our purpose here could be paraphrased like this:

"Peter, do you love me?"

"Yes, Lord, you know that I have warm feelings for you."

"Then feed my sheep."

Jesus' last message to Peter is the last message we need to hear to defeat temptation. In *feed my sheep*, I hear Jesus saying something like this: "Peter, align your desires so that you love me in a way that constructively seeks the good I intend for others—my sheep." The last big insight in *Our Favorite Sins* about winning the battle with temptation is this: one cannot *use* others to satisfy one's desires for sexual titillation or economic gain, and *serve* them too. Lust for the one will toss the other to the curb.

The first decision you need to make as you put this book down is this: What do I really love? The second goes with it: What will I kick to the curb? Answer these two questions and reordering desire will become, over time, automatic. You will find yourself dropping your favorite sins and picking up love for God and your neighbor.

Ancient and Fruitful Practice

The prayer below is variously described as the Methodist Covenant Prayer, the Wesley Covenant Prayer, and a Covenant Prayer in the Wesleyan Tradition.

I am no longer my own, but thine.
Put me to what thou wilt, rank me with whom
thou wilt.
Put me to doing, put me to suffering.
Let me be employed for thee or laid aside for thee,
exalted for thee or brought low for thee.
Let me be full, let me be empty.
Let me have all things, let me have nothing.
I freely and heartily yield all things to thy pleasure
and disposal.
And now, O glorious and blessed God, Father,
Son and Holy Spirit,
thou art mine, and I am thine.
So be it.
And the covenant which I have made on earth,
let it be ratified in heaven.
Amen.[11]

This prayer is a fitting way to complete a book that sets forth reordering desire as the way to defeat temptation. I have the prayer hanging on the door of my office so that

I see it often. With reference to our work in this book, I have found over the years the following lines from this prayer to be most helpful. I suggest you do two things: (1) Go online, find a copy of the prayer, and print it for yourself. Hang it up or carry it around with you until you can feel its heart begin to shape your heart, its spirit form your spirit. (2) For now, just before you put this book down for the last time, pay special attention to the words below from the prayer. Linger with them a bit, considering what the implications might be for such prayers, and take some time to imagine what a life would look like in which these prayers were answered. Here are the sentences I have found most helpful for overcoming temptation:

> *I am no longer my own, but thine . . .*
> *Let me have all things, let me have nothing . . .*
> *I freely and heartily yield all things to thy pleasure*
>   *and disposal . . .*
> *Thou art mine, and I am thine . . .*
> *Amen*

APPENDIX

TEMPTATION BY THE NUMBERS: THE BARNA SURVEY

Introduction

This report contains findings from a nationwide study of adults, ages eighteen years and older, for which the Barna Group conducted online interviews with 1,021 adults nationwide in February 2011. The goals of the survey were

- to identify what temptations Americans face,
- to determine the percentage of Americans who take specific action to try to avoid giving into temptations, and
- to discover what Americans say they do to stay out of tempting situations.

Definitions and Methodology

For purposes of this survey, people are identified as having a practicing faith if they have attended a church service in the past month and say their religious faith is very important in their life. Practicing Protestants are Protestant church attenders who meet the definition for practicing faith; same with Practicing Catholics and Catholic-church attendance.

The survey breaks down across age groups; these are the breakdowns used:

- Mosaics: those currently ages 18 to 26
- Busters: those currently ages 27 to 45
- Boomers: those currently ages 46 to 64
- Elders: those currently ages 65 or older

Regional and ethnic quotas, based upon U.S. Census data sources, were utilized to ensure that the final sample group reflected the distribution of adults nationwide and adequately represented the three primary ethnic groups within the United States (those groups that constitute at least 10 percent of the population: white, black, and Hispanic).

The sampling error for the survey was plus or minus 4 percentage points, at the 95 percent confidence level.

Question 1

Many people say they face temptation, which we could define as being drawn toward doing something that you believe you should not do. How often have you faced each of these temptations in the last month: often, sometimes, not too often, or not at all?

	GENERATION (%)				PRACTICING FAITH (%)	
TOP BOX = Often						
All adults (%)	Mosaic	Buster	Boomer	Elder	Protestant	Catholic
Worrying or being anxious						
23	26	23	26	13	24	7
Procrastinating or putting things off						
20	26	21	20	13	24	20
Eating too much						
17	11	16	19	18	21	17
Spending too much time on media like Internet, television, or video games						
16	19	20	12	11	18	12
Spending more money than you have or can afford						
10	14	12	10	1	9	10
Being lazy or not working as hard as you should						
10	12	11	9	6	11	4
Gossiping or saying mean things about others						
6	11	6	4	3	5	8
Viewing pornography or sexually inappropriate content						
5	6	8	4	2	5	2
Being jealous or envious of others						
4	6	6	2	4	3	4
Lying or cheating						
3	8	2	2	*	2	4
Expressing anger or "going off" on someone online or by text or e-mail						
3	6	4	2	1	5	4
Doing something sexually inappropriate with someone						
3	6	4	1	1	1	1
Abusing alcohol or drugs						
3	5	3	2	1	*	5
n = 1,021	147	349	382	144	182	66

* Less than 0.5%.

	GENERATION (%)				PRACTICING FAITH (%)	
All adults (%)	Mosaic	Buster	Boomer	Elder	Protestant	Catholic
TOP TWO BOXES = Often + Sometimes						
Worrying or being anxious						
60	62	64	59	48	58	57
Procrastinating or putting things off						
60	66	64	60	48	57	51
Eating too much						
55	44	52	62	53	66	44
Spending too much time on media like Internet, television, or video games						
44	53	50	36	38	42	38
Being lazy or not working as hard as you should						
41	56	43	38	30	40	28
Spending more money than you have or can afford						
35	41	39	36	21	34	30
Gossiping or saying mean things about others						
26	37	29	24	13	22	29
Being jealous or envious of others						
24	41	29	19	15	20	24
Viewing pornography or sexually inappropriate content						
18	27	22	15	8	14	16
Lying or cheating						
12	22	14	9	3	12	15
Expressing anger or "going off" on someone online by text or e-mail						
11	25	12	7	5	12	10
Doing something sexually inappropriate with someone						
9	21	11	5	3	5	6
Abusing alcohol or drugs						
11	28	12	6	5	3	9
n = 1,021	147	349	382	144	182	66

Question 2

Think about the last time you faced a temptation of some kind. Did you do anything specific to try to avoid giving in to the temptation?

	GENERATION (%)				PRACTICING FAITH (%)	
All adults (%)	Mosaic	Buster	Boomer	Elder	Protestant	Catholic
Yes	41	35	40	44	43	64	51
No	59	65	60	56	57	36	49
n =	1,021	147	349	382	144	182	66

Question 3

What did you do to try to avoid or stay out of the tempting situation?

	GENERATION (%)				PRACTICING FAITH (%)	
Specific strategies respondents tried to avoid temptation						
All adults (%)	Mosaic	Buster	Boomer	Elder	Protestant	Catholic
Prayed, asked God for help or strength						
18	3	21	15	29	34	23
Used reason and reminders, convinced self, weighed options						
12	26	14	8	10	10	18
Didn't do it, chose not to participate, said no						
10	7	10	8	16	6	9
Avoided it, stayed away from it						
10	4	9	13	6	9	0
Left, got away, went home						
8	16	9	7	3	10	6
Substituted other activities, focused on something else, changed subject						
8	15	10	7	4	9	13
Considered outcome, consequences, effects						
7	8	4	10	7	4	4
Talked to myself, talked myself out of it						
5	7	6	6	4	3	2
Exercised, engaged in physical activity						
5	6	4	8	0	3	3
Talked to someone else, called someone						
4	6	6	2	1	2	1
Occupied myself with work or activities, stayed busy						
4	5	3	6	2	4	4
Took preventative measures						
4	4	4	6	1	3	0
Recalled Scripture, read Bible						
4	4	2	5	3	10	0

Went for a walk	3	4	5	2	1	3	0
Considered impact on others	3	2	4	4	1	1	0
Used willpower, self-control, resistance	3	0	6	2	2	2	0
Thought about something else	3	0	4	2	9	4	0
Listened to music	2	6	3	2	0	*	0
Gave myself time, waited, put it off, slept on it	2	3	1	2	3	0	0
Breathed, counted to ten	2	0	3	2	0	3	0
Read (other than Bible)	2	0	2	3	1	2	0
Stopped activity, backed off, refused to participate	2	2	1	2	5	3	11
Substituted different foods, healthy foods	2	0	2	5	0	4	0
Depended on, reminded myself of faith/God/Christianity	2	0	1	4	1	4	0
Thought better, positive, optimistic thoughts	1	0	2	2	1	0	2
Went to bed	1	0	1	2	0	3	2
Shut my mouth, stayed quiet, held my tongue	1	0	0	2	1	*	1
Placed myself in the company of others, including meetings	1	0	1	2	0	0	2
Other	3	2	4	3	5	3	9
Not sure	2	4	0	4	1	1	5
n =	374	39	122	156	57	104	32

* Less than 0.5%.

243

Question 4

People give in to temptations for many reasons. Which of the following describes the most common reason why you personally give in to temptations?

	GENERATION (%)				PRACTICING FAITH (%)	
Most common reason for giving in to temptations						
All adults (%)	Mosaic	Buster	Boomer	Elder	Protestant	Catholic
I am not really sure						
50	52	46	50	59	46	50
To escape or get away from "real life" for a while						
20	21	24	19	15	13	20
To feel less pain or loneliness						
8	7	10	9	4	10	14
To satisfy people's expectations of me						
7	8	8	5	6	8	8
To take a shortcut to success						
2	2	3	1	4	3	0
Personal pleasure; I enjoy it**						
2	3	2	2	3	2	0
I don't give in to temptations**						
2	1	1	4	2	4	3
Human nature, natural response, sinful nature**						
1	1	1	2	1	4	0
It's easier; too tired or stressed to resist**						
1	1	1	1	2	1	0
I don't have any temptations**						
1	0	2	1	1	1	0
Weakness, not enough self-discipline or willpower**						
1	0	*	1	2	2	1
Other						
4	5	3	6	2	7	4

| n = | 1,021 | 147 | 349 | 382 | 144 | 182 | 66 |

* Less than 0.5%.

** These responses were coded from the write-in response and were not presented to respondents in the questionnaire.

NOTES

Chapter 1: The Tyranny of What You Want

1. Dietrich Bonhoeffer, *Creation and Fall: Temptation* (New York: Macmillan, 1965), 118.
2. Ibid., 116.
3. From *1979 Book of Common Prayer,* 100.

Chapter 2: Disordered Desires

1. Viewed by the author on the premises of the Ritz-Carlton location in Dana Point, CA, March 4, 2011.
2. *The New Dictionary of Christian Ethics and Pastoral Theology,* s.v. "Lust." (Downer's Grove, IL: IVP, 1995), 558.
3. Barna OmniPoll; percentage of Americans who answered *often* and *sometimes.*

4. The Barna Survey is accurate within +/- 3 percent.
5. Barna OmniPoll; percentage of Americans who answered *often* and *sometimes.*
6. Barna survey, 62 percent of Mosaics, but only 48 percent of Elders.
7. Barna OmniPoll; percentage of Americans who answered *often* and *sometimes.*
8. Barna survey, 66 percent of Mosaics, 48 percent of Elders.
9. Barna OmniPoll; percentage of Americans who answered *often* and *sometimes.*
10. Ibid.
11. Barna OmniPoll; percentage of Americans who answered *often* and *sometimes.*
12. I thank R. Kent Hughes in *Victory Over Temptation* for these ideas (Eugene, OR: Harvest House, 1998), 188.
13. C. S. Lewis, *The Screwtape Letters* (New York: Macmillan, 1976), 118.
14. Prayer of Absolution, *1979 Book of Common Prayer.*

Chapter 3: The Insider Report

1. Bonhoeffer, *Creation and Fall,* 112.
2. James K. A. Smith, *Desiring the Kingdom* (Grand Rapids: Baker Books, 2009), 25, 26.
3. Ibid., 40, 54.
4. Ibid., 75.
5. Barna survey.
6. Ibid.
7. Barna study.
8. See the appendix for the complete survey results.
9. See page 242, appendix.
10. Ibid.
11. Ibid.

12. See table on pages 239–40, appendix.

13. *1979 Book of Common Prayer*, Collect for Fifth Sunday in Lent.

Chapter 4: Anxious Annie

1. Bonhoeffer, *Creation and Fall*, 112.

2. I am grateful to my friend Dr. Susan Buckles for her insights on the previous two sentences.

3. Barna research; documents on file.

4. Barna survey.

5. N. T. Wright, *Following Jesus* (Grand Rapids, MI: Eerdmans, 1994), 83.

6. Smith, *Desiring the Kingdom*, 77.

7. Wright, *Following Jesus*, 88.

8. *The New Dictionary of Christian Ethics and Pastoral Theology*, s.v. "Temptation," P. H. Lewis (emphasis added).

Chapter 5: Procrastinating Preston

1. Thanks to Susan Buckles, who helped me create Preston, whose story, like the other character stories in the book, is a fictional amalgam built on real experiences with real people.

2. Barna survey.

3. *The Ancient Christian Commentary on Scripture*, NT, Vol. XI, Ed. Gerald Bray, (Downers Grove, IL: IVP, 2000), 12.

4. J. A. Motyer, *The Message of James* (Downers Grove, IL: IVP, 1985), 50.

5. *The Ancient Christian Commentary on Scripture*, NT, Vol. XI, 12.

6. Collect for Purity, *1979 Book of Common Prayer*.

Chapter 6: Eating Eddie

1. Henri J. M. Nouwen, *The Way of the Heart* (New York: Ballantine Books, 2003), 24.

2. Thanks again to Susan Buckles for helping me to create Eddie.
3. These comments are culled from the Barna survey.
4. Barna survey.
5. Lewis, *The Screwtape Letters*, 41.
6. Dallas Willard, *The Divine Conspiracy* (San Francisco: HarperCollins, 1998), 165, 166.
7. *The New Dictionary of Christian Ethics and Pastoral Theology*, s.v. "Lust."
8. C. S. Lewis, *The Weight of Glory* (San Francisco: HarperCollins, 2001), 26.
9. *Prudentius*, Vol. 1, translated by H. J. Thomson (Cambridge, MA: Harvard Univ. Press, 2006), 235.
10. Lewis, *The Screwtape Letters*, 40.
11. Ibid., 14.
12. The Northumbria Community, *Celtic Daily Prayer: from the Northumbria Community* (San Francisco: HarperOne, 2002), 45.

Chapter 7: Media Mary

1. Corrie Ten Boom, as quoted in *Victory Over Temptation*, 173.
2. This story is composed of many stories known to me, but not the story of one person.
3. These come from the Barna survey.
4. Ibid.
5. http://articles.cnn.com/2009-04-23/health/ ep.facebook.addict_1_facebook-page-facebook-world-social-networking?_s=PM:HEALTH, viewed March 29, 2011.
6. Ibid.
7. Lewis, *The Screwtape Letters*, 42.
8. Ibid., 117.
9. Dallas Willard, *Renovation of the Heart* (Colorado Springs: NavPress, 2002), 119.
10. *Celtic Daily Prayer*, 21.

Chapter 8: Lazy Larry

1. C. S. Lewis, *God in the Dock*, ed. Walter Hooper (Grand Rapids: Eerdmans, 1970), 52. I have a version of this quote on a postcard under the glass that sits atop my desk at work.
2. These attempts at avoiding temptation come from the Barna survey.
3. I am indebted to my friend and colleague Dr. Dennis Okholm for this insight.
4. The origin of the quote is unknown to me.
5. Willard, *Renovation*, 24.
6. Ibid., 22, 23.
7. Dallas Willard, *God and the Problem of Evil*, http://www.dwillard.org/articles/artview.asp?artID=30 (emphasis his).
8. Lewis, *The Screwtape Letters*, 8.
9. Ibid., 10.
10. *Celtic Daily Prayer*, 31.
11. Ibid., 33.

Chapter 9: Modern and Futile

1. Nouwen, *The Way of the Heart*, 11.
2. Thank you to my friend and colleague Dr. Gary Moon for this insight.
3. Thank you to my friend and colleague Dr. Dennis Okholm for this insight.
4. Eighteenth-century hymn "Come Thou Font of Every Blessing," by Robert Robinson.
5. "Dried Up Well" is the title to a song by Mustard Seed Faith, from their 1975 album *Sail On Sailor*.
6. http://snltranscripts.jt.org/85/85bliar.phtml.
7. *Victory Over Temptation*, 100.
8. Willard, *The Divine Conspiracy*, 265.
9. Bonhoeffer, *Creation and Fall*, 98.

10. Michael J. Wilkins, *Matthew The NIV Application Commentary* (Grand Rapids, MI: Zondervan, 2004), 279.
11. *Celtic Daily Prayer*.
12. Ibid., 217.

Chapter 10: Ancient and Fruitful, Part 1

1. Nouwen, *The Way of the Heart*, 13.
2. *Counsels on the Spiritual Life: Mark the Monk*, Vol. 1 and 2 (Crestwood, NY: St. Vladimir's Seminary Press, 2009), 58.
3. Ibid.
4. Ibid., 62, 68.
5. Ibid., 69, 74, 78.
6. Nouwen, *The Way of the Heart*, 16 (emphasis mine).
7. Ibid., 23.
8. Ibid., 35, 45, 48.
9. Ibid., 57.
10. Bonhoeffer, *Creation and Fall*, 111 (emphasis added).
11. Thank you to R. V. G. Tasker for this insight from *The General Epistle of James*, Tyndale New Testament Series (Grand Rapids, MI: Eerdmans, 1977), 46.
12. I owe thanks to George M. Stulac for this insight from *The IVP New Testament Commentary Series, James* (Downers Grove, IL: IVP, 1993), 56.
13. *1979 Book of Common Prayer*, 148.

Chapter 11: Ancient and Fruitful, Part 2

1. William C. Spohn, *Go and Do Likewise* (New York: Continuum, 1999), 154.
2. *The New International Dictionary of New Testament Theology*, Vol.1, s.v. "Desire," H. Schonweiss (Grand Rapids, MI: Zondervan, 1971).
3. I am indebted to my friend Richard Foster, who in a phone

interview for this book suggested this tried-and-true historic pattern for dealing with sin.

4. Timothy Keller, *Counterfeit Gods* (New York: Dutton, 2009), 29.

5. Idaho Springs Inquiries Concerning Spiritual Formation as reprinted in Dallas Willard, *The Great Omission* (San Francisco: HarperCollins, 2006), 103ff.

6. *1979 Book of Common Prayer,* *"Collect of the Day."* It is called *A Collect for the Renewal of Life.*

Chapter 12: Liturgical Prayers and Offices

1. Spohn, *Go and Do Likewise,* 46.

2. *1979 Book of Common Prayer*, 41.

3. Ibid., "The Prayer of Absolution," 360.

4. Nouwen, *The Way of the Heart,* 71.

5. Ibid., 75.

6. Ibid., 82.

7. *1979 Book of Common Prayer*, 148.

8. Ibid., 149.

9. Ibid.

10. *Celtic Daily Prayer,* 19.

11. *1979 Book of Common Prayer*, 219.

12. *1928 Book of Common Prayer*, 54.

13. *Celtic Daily Prayer*, 21.

14. Ibid., 31.

15. Ibid., 33.

16. Ibid., 43.

17. Ibid., 217.

18. *1928 Book of Common Prayer*, 54.

19. *1979 Book of Common Prayer*, 133.

20. *Celtic Daily Prayer*, 16

21. Ibid., 23.

22. *1979 Book of Common Prayer*, 100.

23. *1928 Book of Common Prayer*, 55.

24. *Celtic Daily Prayer, 28, 29.*

25. Ibid., 31.

26. Ibid., 40.

27. Ibid., 41.

28. *1979 Book of Common Prayer*, 355.

29. Ibid., 99.

30. Ibid., 150.

31. *Celtic Daily Prayer*, 38.

32. Ibid., 39.

33. *1979 Book of Common Prayer*, 152.

34. *Celtic Daily Prayer,* 17.

35. Ibid., 18, 19.

36. Ibid., 45.

37. Ibid., 34.

Chapter 13: Sacrament: God Is with Us

1. Spohn, *Go and Do Likewise*, 5.

2. http://cicw.cc/view/partners/rw.php?URL=http://
   www.reformedworship.org/magazine/article.cfm?article_
   id=1988; viewed April 2, 2011.

3. Spohn, *Go and Do Likewise*, 2.

4. Ibid., 3.

5. *1979 Book of Common Prayer*, 302–303.

6. Ibid., "The Holy Eucharist, Rite Two," 362.

7. Ibid., 363.

8. Ibid., 365.

9. Ibid.

10. Viewed at http://www.anglican.org.au/Web/Website.nsf/
    content/Commission:_Liturgy#Holy%20Communion.

11. *Celtic Daily Prayer*, 18, 19.

Chapter 14: The Lectionary: Seeing Sin in Context

1. Max De Pree, *Leading Without Power* (Holland, MI: Shepherd Foundation, 1997), 116.
2. Ibid.
3. Ibid., 171.
4. I first heard this term from my friends John Franke and the late Stanley Grenz. It also occurs in their book *Beyond Foundationalism* (Westminster: John Knox Press, 2001).
5. Spohn, *Go and Do Likewise*, 120.

Conclusion: A New Beginning

1. De Pree, *Leading Without Power*, 151.
2. Isaac Watts, "When I Survey the Wondrous Cross," published in *Hymns and Spiritual Songs* (Hamburg: tradition, 2011), 340.
3. Lewis, *The Screwtape Letters*, 59.
4. Chip Heath and Dan Heath, *Switch* (New York: Broadway Books, 2010), 210.
5. Ibid., 227 (emphasis added).
6. Ibid., 41.
7. Ibid., 207.
8. Quoted in Heath, 144.
9. Lewis, *The Screwtape Letters*, 60 (emphasis added).
10. I am indebted for this idea to Chip and Dan Heath, 6.
11. This prayer is found in numerous sources. Quoted here from http://methodism.org.uk/index.cfm?fuseaction=opentogod. content&cmid=1499.

ACKNOWLEDGMENTS AND SPECIAL THANKS

Writing books imposes strains of various kinds on one's life. The people who feel them most are those closest to the author. In my case that means my two children, Jonathan and Carol, and my deeply loved wife, Debbie. While battling with stage-four cancer, she nevertheless finds the strength to give me away to daily periods of writing. In return, in very many ways, I write for them as my best-loved audience.

My colleagues at Holy Trinity Church, Churches for the Sake of Others, and Telos Events also graciously accept the burden of not having my full attention. I thank them: Rebecca Taylor, Lisa Pompa, Michael Swanson, Scott Pederson,

Dave Ables, Cindy Rethmeier, Paul Martin, Beth Khorey, Joe Randeen, Ellis Brust, Cynthia Brust, Tony Baron, Trish Nelson, Brad Swope, Tony Kriz, Cary Peterson, Ger Jones, Julie Cruz, John Saladino, and Michelle Nanney.

Throughout the writing process David Kinnaman at Barna Research was more than just a vendor of statistics. David is a friend and was a wise and helpful companion along the way, helping the book take shape.

Dennis Okholm, Susan Buckles, Tom Carmody, and Pat Coneen, four intelligent friends at Holy Trinity Church, read the manuscript for me and offered constructive criticism that resulted in a better book than I could have written on my own.

As the concept for this book was taking shape, I wanted to ensure that I covered the topic of temptation well. To head down that path with a solid and reliable map in hand, I interviewed several friends on the topic: Gary Moon, Richard Foster, Chris Webb, Eugene Peterson, Dallas Willard, and James Bryan Smith. Don't blame them for any mistakes herein, but be sure to give them lots of praise for anything helpful!

Finally I must thank Joel Miller, vice president of editorial and acquisitions for the nonfiction division of Thomas Nelson. This book emerged in dialogue between Joel and me, but it would not have happened without his initiative, enthusiasm, and expert guidance. I respect and cherish editorial help. I love making new friends. In Joel I found the best of both worlds.

ABOUT THE AUTHOR

*Todd Hunter is an Anglican bishop and the founding pas-*tor of Holy Trinity Anglican Church. He is an adjunct professor at several seminaries and the author of *Christianity Beyond Belief, Giving Church Another Chance, The Outsider Interviews,* and *The Accidental Anglican.* Todd lives and works in Costa Mesa, California, with his wife, Debbie, and two grown children.